Practice and Procedure in the Sheriff's Ordinary Court

Fourmat Publishing

Lawyers Practice and Procedure Series

Practice and Procedure in the
Sheriff's Ordinary Court
by
D B White,
Sheriff Clerk, Edinburgh

London
Fourmat Publishing
1988

ISBN 1 85190 037 3

First published January 1988

© 1988 Fourmat Publishing
27 & 28 St Albans Place Islington Green London N1 ONX
Printed and bound in Great Britain
by Billings & Sons Limited, Worcester.

Preface

Civil business in the sheriff court falls into several categories - ordinary causes (including divorce); summary causes; miscellaneous applications such as bankruptcy, adoption of children, registration of clubs etc; and commissary (probate) business. The bulk of civil business is dealt with in the Ordinary Court and the Summary Cause Court.

The Sheriff's Ordinary Court, although not the busiest in terms of volume, is the most important civil court in the sheriff court. The jurisdiction of the sheriff's ordinary court is similar to that of the Outer House of the Court of Session, the main exceptions being actions relating to nullity of marriage, reduction, and proving the tenor of a document.

The Ordinary Cause Rules are contained in the Schedule to the Sheriff Courts (Scotland) Act 1907. The first major revision of the rules was enacted in 1983. Further amendments followed the introduction of divorce jurisdiction to the sheriff court, the implementation of the Civil Jurisdiction and Judgments Act 1982 and various family law statutes.

The following text deals with jurisdiction in the sheriff's ordinary court, and the types of action raised in court; it also includes a commentary on the rules and the forms prescribed under the rules. All amendments to the rules and forms up to 1 September 1987 have been taken into account.

DBW
October 1987

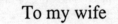
To my wife

Contents

Chapter 1

Jurisdiction

Jurisdiction in ordinary actions is based upon:
  (i)   the location of the pursuer or defender; and/or
  (ii) the nature of the action,
and is regulated by various enactments.

The majority of ordinary actions are covered by the provisions of the Civil Jurisdiction and Judgments Act 1982 which largely replaced s 6 of the Sheriff Courts (Scotland) Act 1907. Certain types of action, mainly consistorial, are excluded from the provisions of the 1982 Act and are covered by other Acts including:
  (i)   the Domicile and Matrimonial Proceedings Act 1973;
  (ii) the Law Reform (Parent and Child) (Scotland) Act 1986; and
  (iii) the Family Law Act 1986.

The grounds of jurisdiction under the Civil Jurisdiction and Judgments Act 1982 are set out in Sch 8 of the Act and consist of:
  (i)   domicile;
  (ii) special jurisdiction;
  (iii) consumer contracts;
  (iv) exclusive jurisdiction; and
  (v)   prorogation.

These are considered in turn below.

1. Domicile

Domicile is the principal ground of jurisdiction under the 1982 Act, which provides that "persons shall be sued in the courts for the place where they are domiciled". So far as ordinary actions are concerned, this will generally mean the sheriff court of the district in which the defender resides or carries on business.

Domicile is defined in the Act. In the case of an individual he is held to be domiciled in Scotland if:
  (i)   he is resident in Scotland; and
  (ii) the nature and circumstance of the residence indicate that he has a substantial connection with Scotland.
So far as (ii) is concerned, residence in Scotland for three months is enough to indicate a substantial connection.

Having established that the individual defender is domiciled in Scotland, the action may be raised in the sheriff court of the sheriff court district in which he is resident.

In the case of corporations and associations, the seat of the corporation or associaton is treated as its domicile. The sheriff has jurisdiction over a corporation or association if:
  (i)   it has its seat in the United Kingdom; and
  (ii) it has its seat in Scotland; and
  (iii) it has its seat in the sheriff court district.

A corporation has its seat in the United Kingdom if:
  (i)   it was incorporated or formed under the law of a part of the United Kingdom and has its registered office or some other official address in the United Kingdom; or
  (ii) its central management or control is exercised in the United Kingdom.

It has its seat in Scotland if:
  (i)   it has its seat in the United Kingdom; and
  (ii) it has its registered office or some other official address in Scotland; or
  (iii) its central management or control, is exercised in Scotland; or
  (iv) it has a place of business in Scotland.

It has its seat in the sheriffdom if:
  (i)   it has its seat in Scotland; and
  (ii) it has its registered office or some other official address in the sheriffdom; or
  (iii) its central management or control is exercised in the

      sheriffdom; or

(iv) it has a place of business in the sheriffdom.

The location of the registered office, other official address or place of business determines the sheriff court in which the action may be raised.

2. Special jurisdiction

The following grounds of special jurisdiction are additional to those under domicile (above) but subject to jurisdiction over consumer contracts, exclusive jurisdiction and prorogation of jurisdiction (below).

(a)   *Contract*

In matters relating to a contract the action may be raised in the sheriff court for the place of performance of the obligation in question. Where the action relates to non-payment of sums due under the contract, the action should be raised in the sheriff court in whose jurisdiction the sums ought to have been paid. Where the action relates to non-performance, the action should be raised in the sheriff court in whose jurisdiction performance ought to have been made.

(b)   *Delict or quasi-delict*

In matters relating to delict or quasi-delict the action may be raised in the sheriff court in whose jurisdiction the harmful event occurred.

(c)   *Maintenance*

Actions relating to maintenance, other than those ancillary to actions affecting status, may be raised in the sheriff court for the place in which the maintenance creditor is domiciled or habitually resident.

Actions relating to maintenance matters ancillary to proceedings concerning status may be raised in the sheriff court which has jurisdiction to entertain those proceedings.

(d)   *Branch, agency etc*

Actions relating to a dispute arising out of the operations of a branch, agency or other establishment may be raised in the sheriff court for the place in which the branch, agency or other establishment is situated.

(e)   Arrestment

This ground of special jurisdiction does not apply to defenders domiciled in EEC Member states (including the United Kingdom) except Greece, Spain and Portugal. It applies to actions raised in the sheriff courts for the place where:
    (i)   any moveable property belonging to the defender has been arrested; or
    ii)   any immoveable property in which he has any beneficial interest is situated.

(f)   Moveable property

Actions to:
    (i)   arrest, declare or determine proprietory or possessory rights or rights in security in or over moveable property; or
    (ii)   obtain authority to dispose of moveable property
may be raised in the sheriff court for the place where the property is situated.

(g)   Interdict

Actions for interdict may be raised in the sheriff court for the place where it is alleged that the wrong is likely to be committed.

(h)   Secured debts

Actions concerning a debt secured over immoveable property may be raised in the sheriff court for the place where the property is situated.

(i)   Decisions of companies etc

Actions which have as their object a decision of an organ of a company or other legal person or of an association may be brought in the sheriff court for the place where that company has its seat.

(j)   More than one defender

A defender who is one of a number of defenders may be sued in the sheriff court for the place where any one of them is domiciled.

(k)   Third party claims

A person may be sued as a third party in an action on a warranty or guarantee or any third party proceedings in the sheriff court hearing the original proceedings. However, this ground of jurisdiction does not apply if the sole purpose of raising the original action was to make the third party subject to the jurisdiction of the court and remove him from the jurisdiction of the court to which he would otherwise be subject.

(l)   Counterclaim

A person may be sued on a counterclaim arising from the same contract or facts on which the original claim was based, in the sheriff court in which the original claim is pending.

3. Consumer contracts

This ground of jurisdiction is restricted to actions in which the contract was concluded by a person for a purpose which can be regarded as being outside his trade or profession. The following conditions have to be satisfied:

  (i)   the contract has to be for the sale of goods on instalment credit terms; or
  (ii) the contract has to be for a loan repayable by instalments or for any other form of credit made to finance the sale of goods; or
  (iii) if, in any other contract for the supply of goods or services:
    •   the consumer took in Scotland the steps necessary for the conclusion of the contract; or
    •   the action is raised in the sheriff court for the place in which the consumer is domiciled.

The consumer has a choice of courts in which he may raise an action. It may be raised in:

(i)   the court for the place in which the other party is domiciled; or

(ii) the court for the place in which he himself is domiciled; or

(iii) any court having jurisdiction as described in *(d)* or *(f)* above.

The other party may raise an action against the consumer only in:

(i)   the court for the place where the consumer is domiciled, or

(ii) any court having jurisdiction as described in *(f)* above,

but has a right to bring a counterclaim in the court in which the original action in relation to the consumer contract is pending.

Parties may agree to prorogate the jurisdiction of the court, but only if:

(i)   the agreement is entered into after the dispute has arisen; or

(ii) the consumer is allowed to raise the action in another court.

4. Exclusive jurisdiction

There are four types of action in which particular sheriff courts have exclusive jurisdiction and in which domicile or any other ground of jurisdiction do not apply:

(i)   proceedings which have as their object rights *in rem* in, or tenancies of, immoveable property must be raised in the sheriff court of the sheriff court district in which the property is situated;

(ii) proceedings which have as their object the validity of the constitution, the nullity or the dissolution of companies or other legal persons or associations of natural or legal persons must be raised in the sheriff court of the sheriff court district in which the company, legal person or association has its seat;

(iii) proceedings which have as their object the validity of entries in public registers must be raised in the sheriff court of the sheriff court district in which the register is kept; and

(iv) proceedings concerned with the enforcement of judgments must be raised in the sheriff court of the sheriff court district in which the judgment has been or is to be enforced.

5. Prorogation of jurisdiction

The sheriff court which parties have agreed is to have jurisdiction to settle any disputes which have arisen or which may arise in connection with a particular legal relationship shall have exclusive jurisdiction except:

(i) where restrictions apply in relation to consumer contracts (see page 17);

(ii) where exclusive jurisdiction has been conferred on a sheriff court (see page 18).

6. Averments in the initial writ

Initial writs in actions to which the Civil Jurisdiction and Judgments Act 1982 applies must contain articles of condescendence stating:

(i) the domicile of the defender as determined in accordance with ss 41 to 46 of, and art 52 of Sch 1 to, the Civil Jurisdiction and Judgments Act 1982; and

(ii) the ground of jurisdiction of the court.

(see r 3, page 26).

The Sheriff shall not grant decree in absence unless it appears *ex facie* of the initial writ that a ground of jurisdiction exists under the 1982 Act (see r 21, page 43).

7. Domicile and Matrimonial Proceedings Act 1973

Jurisdiction in actions for separation or divorce is governed by s 8 of the above Act which provides that an action may be raised in a sheriff court if:

(i) either party to the marriage in question is:

• domiciled in Scotland at the date when the action is begun, or

• was habitually resident there throughout the period of one year ending with that date; and

(ii) either party to the marriage:

• was resident in the sheriffdom for a period of forty days ending with that date; or

19

- had been resident in the sheriffdom for a period of not less than forty days ending not more than forty days before that date and has no known residence in Scotland at that date.

In practice, the action may be raised in the sheriff court of the sheriff court district in which the address of the party establishing jurisdiction is located.

8. Law Reform (Parent and Child) (Scotland) Act 1986

Section 7 of the above Act provides that an action for declarator of parentage, non-parentage, legitimacy, legitimation or illegitimacy may be brought in the sheriff court if:
(i) the child was born in the sheriffdom; or
(ii) the circumstances are such that the action could have been raised in the Court of Session and the alleged or presumed parent or the child was habitually resident in the sheriffdom on the date when the action is brought or on the date of his death.

9. Family Law Act 1986

Chapter 3 of Part I of this Act deals with jurisdiction of courts in Scotland in relation to child custody orders, otherwise than in matrimonial proceedings. The sheriff has jurisdiction to deal with such cases if, on the date of the application:
(i) the child concerned is habitually resident in the sheriffdom; or
(ii) • the child is present in Scotland;
- the child is not habitually resident in any part of the United Kingdom; and
- either the pursuer or the defender is habitually resident in the sheriffdom.

The sheriff also has jurisdiction to deal with emergency applications where:
(i) the child concerned is present in the sheriffdom on the date of the application; and
(ii) the sheriff considers that, for the protection of the child, it is necessary to make a custody order immediately.

Chapter 2

Classification of causes

The term "ordinary cause" (or "ordinary action") is not defined in the Sheriff Courts (Scotland) Act 1907. Business in the sheriff's civil court is divided into the following categories:
(i)   summary causes;
(ii) summary applications; and
(iii) ordinary causes.

The summary cause court deals with actions:
(i)   in which the monetary value does not exceed £1000; or
(ii) for the recovery of possession of heritable property let for less than a year.

Summary applications are defined, in s 3(p) of the 1907 Act, as:
"all applications of a summary nature brought under the common law jurisdiction of the Sheriff, and all applications, whether by appeal or otherwise, brought under any Act of Parliament which provides, or according to any practice in the Sheriff Court, which allows that the same shall be disposed of in a summary manner, but which does not more particularly define in what form the same shall be heard, tried and determined."

All other actions are ordinary causes, the main classifications of which are described below, although this is not exhaustive.

1. Payment

Actions for payment are generally raised for the recovery of a debt for:
(i)   goods supplied;
(ii) services rendered; or

(iii) money given under a loan or IOU.

2. Delict

Actions for delict (to remedy a legal wrong) may be classed under (a) damages or (b) reparation. The range is wide but includes the following actions:

(i) damages for:
- damage to goods in transit;
- infringement of copyright;
- breach of contract;
- trespass;
- failure to complete work; and

(ii) reparation for:
- wrongful arrest;
- breach of arrestment;
- assault;
- fraud;
- negligent performance of work;
- personal injury arising from road traffic accidents, medical treatment;
- breach of promise of marriage.

3. Consistorial

Consistorial actions deal with matters arising from family circumstances and relationships and include:
- divorce;
- separation;
- custody of children;
- access to children;
- delivery of children;
- aliment and periodical allowance; and
- applications under the Matrimonial Homes (Family Protection) (Scotland) Act 1981.

4. Affiliation and aliment

This is an action for declarator which asks the sheriff to establish the paternity of an illegitimate child and normally includes a crave for aliment for the child.

5. Accountancy

The most common action under this heading is one of count, reckoning and payment against a co-partner following dissolution of the partnership.

6. Contract

Actions under this heading include those for implement of or in respect of breach of contract.

7. Declarator

Apart from actions of declarator of marriage or nullity of marriage, which must be raised in the Court of Session, all other actions of declaration may be raised in the ordinary court. The range is wide but includes actions to find and declare that:
  (i)   a will is valid;
  (ii) a right of way exists;
  (iii) a building society has the right to enter into possession of heritable property; and
  (iv) the pursuer has exclusive right to a trade mark.

8. Delivery

Actions for delivery normally relate to inanimate objects such as a purchased article, title deeds, and are often combined with a crave for payment as an alternative, but they may also relate to delivery of a child.

9. Division and sale of heritable property

Actions under this heading are rare. Their purpose is to ask the sheriff to decide which portions of heritable property belong to joint proprietors and to authorise the sale of the property and the division of proceeds.

10. Actions of furthcoming

Moveable property belonging to a debtor may be arrested in the hands of a third party. If the debtor does not authorise the release of the property, an action of furthcoming is raised by the creditor.

11. Implement

An action of implement is a remedy when a party to a contract fails or refuses to fulfil an obligation under the contract.

12. Interdict

An action of interdict may be raised in respect of an alleged wrong being committed or threatened to be committed and includes such matters as:
* access to premises;
* infringement of copyright;
* use of a trade name;
* trespass; and
* diversion of a water supply.

13. Multiplepoinding

An action of multiplepoinding may be raised when there are two or more competing claims on a fund *in medio* which may comprise moveable or heritable property. It may be raised by a claimant on the fund or by the holder of the fund. For example, if, following a criminal trial, there are competing claims to ownership of property held by the Procurator Fiscal, an action may be raised by one or more of the claimants, or the Procurator Fiscal may raise the action so that the sheriff may determine ownership.

14. Partnership

An ordinary action of declarator may be raised to find and declare that a partnership is at an end and should be dissolved.

15. Removing

The most common ordinary action of removing is that against a defender without a title, eg a squatter. An action of declarator of irritancy and removing may be raised by a superior against a vassal (see r 103, page 95).

Chapter 3

Commencement of the case

1. The initial writ (r 3)

All ordinary causes are commenced by initial writ which is defined as:

> "the statement of claim, petition, note of appeal or other document by which the action is initiated."
> (Sheriff Courts (Scotland) Act 1907 s 3(k)).

Its form must be as nearly as may be in accordance with Form A in the Appendix to the Ordinary Cause Rules (see page 134).

The initial writ must contain a statement, in numbered paragraphs, of the facts which form the grounds of the action. The statement is known as the condescendence. This requirement applies to all initial writs, but specific articles of condescendence are required in relation to jurisdiction in the following circumstances:

   (i) *prorogation* - if the pursuer has reason to believe that an agreement may exist prorogating the jurisdiction over the subject matter of the cause to another court, the initial writ must contain an averment to that effect but there is no requirement to insert a negative averment;

   (ii) *pending proceedings* - if the pursuer has reason to believe that proceedings may be pending before another court involving the same cause or action and between the same parties as those named in the initial writ, the initial writ must contain an averment to that effect, but there is no requirement to insert a negative averment.

   (iii) an article of condescendence must be included stating:
   • the domicile of the defender; and

- the grounds of jurisdiction of the court.
(see also page 13 as to jurisdiction).

In actions of divorce or of separation it is obligatory to insert an article of condescendence specifying whether any proceedings are continuing (ie not finally disposed of) in Scotland or elsewhere in respect of the marriage to which the initial writ relates. If there are proceedings which are continuing, the articles of condescendence must specify:

(i) the court, tribunal or authority before which they have been commenced;

(ii) the date of commencement;

(iii) the names of the parties;

(iv) whether a proof or hearing has been appointed and, if so, the date; and

(v) any other facts which might assist the sheriff to determine whether the action before him should be sisted in terms of Sch 3 to the Domicile and Matrimonial Proceedings Act 1973.

(Information about continuing proceedings, as mentioned above, must also be inserted in any defences or minutes lodged by any party if it is additional to or contradictory of the information provided by the pursuer, or if the pursuer has provided no such information.)

Applications under the Domicile and Matrimonial Proceedings Act 1973 by a party in an action of divorce or of separation:

(i) for an order under Sch 2 of the 1973 Act (such as interim aliment or regulating the custody of children); or

(ii) for a sist or recall of a sist under Sch 3 of the 1973 Act (because proceedings in respect of the marriage are proceeding in another jurisdiction),

must be made by written motion.

Where an initial writ in an action of divorce is presented to the sheriff clerk it must be accompanied by:

(i) an extract of the relevant entry in the register of marriages; and

(ii) where appropriate, an extract of the relevant entry in the register of births.

A warrant to cite will not be granted if the necessary documents are not presented, unless the sheriff, on cause shewn, otherwise directs.

Section 47 of the Children Act 1975 provides for an application relating to the custody of a child to be made by any relative, step-parent or foster parent of the child. In such cases:

    (i)   the parents of the child must be called as defenders and, if their address is known, citation and service must be effected in accordance with the rules (see also r 130, page 112); and

    (ii) the consent of a parent, tutor, curator or guardian, in terms of Form T1 in the Schedule to the Rules, must be lodged.

2. Signature and backing (r 4)

The initial writ must be signed by the pursuer or his solicitor and the name and address of the solicitor, if any, must be stated on the back of every service copy.

Form A in the Schedule to the Rules requires the signature of the pursuer or his solicitor only at the end of the crave, but, in practice, the writ is also signed after the pleas-in-law.

3. Warrant of citation (r 5)

When the initial writ has been presented to the sheriff clerk, the normal first procedure is for the grant of a warrant to cite the defender (to inform him that he is being sued and to provide him with a copy of the initial writ). The warrant of citation is in terms of Form B in the Appendix to the Ordinary Cause Rules except in actions of divorce or of separation, in which cases the warrant is in terms of Form B1. See page 134 for forms.

4. Arrestment to found jurisdiction (r 6)

It may be necessary to execute an arrestment to found jurisdiction against the defender, ie arrestment of moveable property belonging to the defender, or immoveable property in which he has a beneficial interest, and located within the court's jurisdiction, for the purpose of giving the court jurisdiction over the defender (see page 16). In such a case, application may be made in the initial writ, but there must be averments in the condescendence to justify granting the warrant. This procedure is restricted to defenders who are domiciled furth of the United Kingdom and the EEC.

Chapter 4

Citation and service

1. Introduction

In most ordinary causes, the defender resides in Scotland and the standard method of service is by recorded delivery post by the pursuer's solicitor. Normally, it is only where postal service has failed, for example because there is no answer, that alternative methods are used. The pursuer's solicitor instructs a sheriff officer to effect service, either by delivering the service copy document personally or by leaving a copy with a responsible person; or, failing personal contact, by leaving or affixing the service copy at the address - sometimes known as "keyhole citation".

Special provisions apply in cases of divorce or separation where the defender is suffering from a mental disorder or his whereabouts are unknown, and on persons resident outwith Scotland.

2. Period of notice (r 7)

In all ordinary actions there is a period of time, following citation and before the case is returned to court, in which the defender may consider his position, take legal advice etc. This is known as the period of notice. The length of the period varies depending on where the defender is resident or has a place of business. The periods are:
  (i)   14 days when the defender resides in or has a place of business in the United Kingdom, the Isle of Man, the Channel Islands or the Republic of Ireland;
  (ii) 28 days when the defender is resident or has a place of business outside the United Kingdom, Isle of Man, the Channel Islands or the Republic of Ireland but is resident or has a place of business elsewhere in Europe; and

(iii) 42 days when the defender is resident or has a place of business outside Europe.

The above periods may be shortened or extended by the sheriff, on cause shown by the pursuer, but a minimum of two days notice must be given.

In fairness to the defender, where the period of notice expires on a Saturday, Sunday, public or court holiday, the period of notice is deemed to expire on the first following day on which the sheriff clerk's office is open for civil court business.

3. Signature of warrants (r 8)

In the majority of cases, warrants for citation of the defender or for arrestment on the dependence (of the action) are signed by the sheriff clerk or one of his deputes. However, the sheriff may sign any warrant and only he may sign a warrant containing an order shortening or extending the period of notice.

The sheriff clerk will normally satisfy himself of the *prima facie* competence of the initial writ. If he is not satisfied, and declines to sign a warrant for citation, the initial writ may be presented to the sheriff for his consideration.

4. Form of citation and certificate (r 9)

Except where the address of the defender is unknown (see r 11 below), citation of the defender is carried out by serving him with a notice in terms of Form C in the Schedule to the rules, except in actions of divorce or of separation, in which cases Form C1 is used. See pages 135 and 136 for the forms. The notice is prefixed to a copy of the initial writ (the service copy) and the warrant of citation and, in the cases of divorce and separation, any forms specified in r 131.

The defender having been cited, the person executing the citation signs a certificate in terms of Form D in the schedule to the rules.

Most citations are served by post by a solicitor. Officers of court, ie sheriff officers, may serve citations by post. In either case, the person executing the citation must sign a certificate in terms of Form D in the schedule to the rules.

Service otherwise than by post may only be executed by an officer of court (see r 10). In this case a witness is necessary, the certificate must be signed by the officer and the witness and the mode of citation must be specified, together with the name of any person to whom the citation was delivered by the officer.

5. Service in Scotland by officer of the court (r 10)

In ordinary cause procedure, various documents may have to be served on persons connected with the cause. Any initial writ, decree, charge, warrant or other order or writ may be served by an officer of court on any person:

(i)   personally; or
(ii)   by leaving it in the hands of an inmate of or employee at the person's dwelling place or place of business.

If the officer is unsuccessful in effecting service by either of these methods he may, after making diligent inquiries, serve the document either:

(i)   by depositing it in the dwelling place or place of business, via the letter box or by other lawful means; or
(ii)   by affixing it to the door of the dwelling place or place of business,

and in these cases the officer must, as soon as possible afterwards, send a copy of the document by ordinary post to the address at which he thinks it most likely that the person may be found.

Where an officer effects service by letter box or by affixing, the certificate referred to under r 9 must contain a statement of the mode of service previously attempted, the circumstances which prevented such service, and a statement that a copy of the document was sent to the address at which the officer thinks it most likely that the person may be found.

6. Citation of persons whose address is unknown (r 11)

In ordinary actions (other than actions of divorce or of separation where either the defender's address is unknown or the defender is suffering from mental disorder, in which cases, see r 11A below) in which the defender's address is unknown, the sheriff must grant warrant to cite the defender:

(i) by publication of an advertisement in terms of Form E in the schedule to the rules, in a newspaper circulating in the area of the defender's last known address; or

(ii) by displaying a copy of the instance and crave of the initial writ, warrant of citation and a notice in terms of Form E1 in the schedule to the Rules, on the Walls of Court.

The period of notice (fixed by the sheriff) runs from the date of publication of the advertisement or display on the Walls of Court. The documents to be displayed on the Walls of Court and the service copy for the defender must be lodged with the sheriff clerk by the pursuer.

The following documents must be lodged with the sheriff clerk by the pursuer:

(i) a certified copy of the instance and crave of the initial writ and the warrant of citation (where display on the Walls of Court is required);

(ii) a service copy of the initial writ and a copy of the warrant of citation (for possible collection by the defender); and

(iii) where appropriate, a copy of the newspaper containing the advertisement as evidence of publication.

If, following citation by newspaper advertisement or display on the Walls of Court, and after the cause has commenced, the defender's address becomes known, the sheriff may review the procedure, allow the initial writ to be amended and make orders relating to re-service of the writ, intimation, expenses or transfer of the cause, as he thinks fit.

7. Intimation in actions of divorce or separation - defender suffering from mental disorder or address unknown (r 11A)

Apart from the exception mentioned below, the procedure in actions in which the defender is suffering from a mental disorder within the meaning of the Mental Health (Scotland) Act 1980, or the defender's address is unknown, is similar. The warrant of citation must include an order for intimation to:

(i) every child of the marriage who has reached the age of 12 years in the case of a girl and 14 years in the case of a boy;

(ii) one of the defender's next-of-kin who has reached the above age; and

(iii) the curator *bonis* to the defender (if any),

unless it is stated in the initial writ that the address of any such person is unknown.

Intimation to such persons is made in terms of Form VI in the Schedule to the Rules (where the defender is suffering from mental disorder) or Form V2 (where the defender's whereabouts are unknown). Any person receiving such notice may apply, within the period of notice, by minute craving to be sisted as a party, for leave to lodge defences or answers as the case may be.

If the defender is resident in a hospital or similar institution, the citation is sent by post to the medical officer in charge and is accompanied by a request in terms of Form W in the Schedule to the Rules that the medical officer deliver the service copy initial writ to the defender personally and explain the purpose of the writ unless satisfied that to do so would be dangerous to the health or mental condition of the defender. In terms of Form W, the medical officer is requested to complete and return to the pursuer's solicitor a certificate, in terms of Form V in the Schedule to the Rules, as to whether or not the copy writ has been delivered to the defender. If the medical officer has decided not to serve the copy initial writ, and has completed the certificate to that effect, the sheriff may order further medical enquiry and such service of the initial writ as he thinks fit.

See pages 153 to 155 for the forms.

8. Citation of or service on persons outwith Scotland (r 12)

The method of service on persons outwith Scotland depends on the residence or place of business or location of the persons. It also depends on whether or not a Convention on the service of documents exists between the United Kingdom and the country concerned. Sheriff clerks will advise on the existence of a Convention. See also page 13 on jurisdiction.

(a) *Methods of service*

Where a person has a known residence or place of business in:
- England;
- Wales;
- Northern Ireland;
- The Isle of Man;
- The Channel Islands; or
- any country with which the United Kingdom does not have a Convention providing for the service of writs,

service is effected by:
(i) personal service in accordance with the domestic law of the country concerned; or
(ii) postal service in Scotland by registered or recorded delivery post or the nearest equivalent.

Where a person is located in a country which is a party to the Hague Convention or the European Convention, ie:
- Belgium;
- Denmark;
- France;
- Luxembourg;
- Netherlands;
- West Germany; and
- Italy,

service may be effected by one of the following methods:
(i)   by the method prescribed by the internal law of the country;
(ii) by requesting the Foreign Office to arrange service;
(iii) where the law of the country permits, by postal service in Scotland by registered or recorded delivery post or the nearest equivalent; or
(iv) where the law of the country permits, by the equivalent of a sheriff officer.

Where a person is located in a country with which the United Kingdom has a Convention on the service of writs, other than the Hague

Convention or the European Convention, service may be effected by one of the methods approved in the Convention.

(b)   Translation

If English is not an official language in the country in which service is to be effected, all documents to be served must be accompanied by a translation into the language of the country. The translation must be certified correct by the translator whose full name, address and qualifications must be included in a certificate lodged with the execution of citation or certificate of execution.

(c)   Postal service

The procedure for postal service is similar to that for persons resident or carrying on business in Scotland (see page 32 above). Service may be effected by a solicitor or a sheriff officer. The covering envelope must bear the same wording as is specified in r 15(3) (see page 38), but also there must be a translation of the wording into the language of the country if appropriate.

(d)   Foreign Office

Where service is to be effected through:
     (i)   a central authority in the country; or
     (ii)   a British Consular authority,
at the request of the Foreign Office, a copy of the writ and warrant with citation attached (and a translation), with a request for service to be effected, should be sent to the Secretary of State for Foreign and Commonwealth Affairs. A certificate of execution of service by the authority which has effected service must be obtained and lodged in process.

(e)   Sheriff officer equivalent

Where service is to be effected by the equivalent of a sheriff officer, the pursuer, his solicitor or the sheriff officer must send to the official in the country a copy of the writ and warrant for service with citation attached (and a translation), with a request for service to be effected by delivery to the defender or his residence. A certificate of execution of service must be obtained and lodged in process.

(f)   Personal service

Where personal service is effected, the pursuer must lodge a certificate by a person who is conversant with the law of the country concerned, stating that the form of service is in accordance with the law of the country concerned. Such a certificate is unnecessary if service has taken place in another part of the United Kingdom, the Channel Islands or the Isle of Man.

9. Days of charge (r 13)

As a general rule, the defender in an action must be given written notice by a sheriff officer that a decree has been granted or an order has been made against him and that a period of time must expire before the decree or order can be enforced. In ordinary causes, the period is 14 days.

10. Persons carrying on business under a trading or descriptive name (r 14)

Any person or persons carrying on a business under a trading or descriptive name, may sue or be sued in such trading or descriptive name alone.

Any extract of a decree:
 (i)   pronounced in the sheriff court; or
 (ii) proceeding upon any document recorded in the sheriff court books in which execution may competently proceed
against such person or persons, under such trading or descriptive name, is a valid warrant for diligence against such person or persons.

Service of any document to which this rule applies is made at any place of business or office at which such business is carried on in the sheriffdom of the sheriff court in which the cause is brought or, if there is no place of business in the sheriffdom, service may be effected at any place (including the place of business or office of the clerk or secretary of any company corporation or association or firm) where such business is carried on.

11. Postal citation (r 15)

Postal citation or service is by far the most common mode in ordinary causes. Although it is competent to use registered post, the normal method is by recorded delivery, in which case it must be by first class mail.

When postal service is used, the period of notice starts to run on the day of posting.

The following notice must be printed or written on the face of the envelope sent by post:
"This letter contains a citation to or intimation from .... Sheriff Court. If delivery of the letter cannot be made at the address shown it is to be returned immediately to The Sheriff Clerk, Sheriff Court, ..."

The receipt issued by the Post Office must be attached to the certificate of citation.

12. Endorsation unnecessary (r 16)

In Scotland, any initial writ, decree etc may be served outside the jurisdiction of the originating sheriff court without the need to obtain an endorsation by the sheriff court within whose jurisdiction the document is to be served; and it may be served by an officer of the court of the originating court or of the sheriff court district within which it is to be executed.

13. Re-service (r 17)

If the sheriff is satisfied that service of an initial writ on the defender has not been properly carried out, he may order the initial writ to be re-served. Normally, a warrant for re-service is craved, and granted, when an attempt at citation has been made and failed. The sheriff may not be satisfied with the reason given and may grant warrant for re-service, upon such conditions as seem just.

14. Personal bar (r 18)

Irregularities in service can be corrected by re-serving the initial writ but a party who appears in answer to the citation forfeits any right to challenge any irregularity in service. However, he is not barred from pleading that the court has no jurisdiction.

15. Dispensing powers (r 1)

The Ordinary Cause Rules include directions to parties to carry out certain actions, sometimes within prescribed time limits, for instance to lodge a notice of intention to defend within a period of notice of 14 days. In some cases, such as the grant of decree in absence of the defender, the rules provide a specific remedy for the failure of a party to observe time limits. Where the rules do not so provide, the sheriff has a wide discretion to relieve any party from the consequences of failure to comply with the rules.

If the sheriff is satisfied that there was good reason for the failure, and that there was no wilful non-observance of the rules, he may exercise his dispensing powers on such terms and conditions as he considers just. The dispensing order specifies the action to be taken to bring procedure within the rules and, that having been done, the case proceeds as if the failure had not happened.

16. Application of rules to solicitors

With few exceptions (for example r 97; see page 91), the rules make no mention of solicitors, albeit the vast majority of ordinary causes are conducted by solicitors. Any reference to a party in the rules (eg pursuer) should, where appropriate, be construed as a reference to the solicitor representing that party.

Chapter 5

Transfer of causes

1. Transfer to another sheriff court (r 19)

The sheriff has wide powers to transfer an ordinary cause from his own sheriff court to another. There are three ways in which transfer is effected:

(i) where there are two or more defenders and the action has been raised in the sheriff court district in which one defender resides or carries on business, the cause may be transferred to another sheriff court having jurisdiction over one of the defenders;

(ii) where a plea of no jurisdiction has been sustained and the cause is remitted to the sheriff court before which it appears that it ought to have been raised;

(iii) where, on cause shewn, the sheriff decides to remit the cause to another sheriff court, irrespective of jurisdiction.

In cases (i) and (ii), the sheriff may only transfer the cause on the motion of one or more of the parties, but he has an overriding power to transfer if he is satisfied that there is sufficient cause. Transfer of causes is mostly made under head (iii) above, either because parties and/or witnesses reside in a sheriff court district other than that in which the action has been raised or because a connected action is pending before the other sheriff court.

On making the transfer the sheriff must state his reasons in the interlocutor and may make such order on expenses as he thinks fit.

The receiving court must accept the transfer and the cause proceeds as if it has been raised in that court.

The interlocutor is appealable to the Sheriff Principal, with leave of the sheriff, but not beyond (see also r 92, page 88).

2. Remit to the Court of Session (r 20)

The sheriff court has privative (exclusive) jurisdiction to deal with all causes not exceeding £500 in value exclusive of interest and expenses (s 7 1907 Act). However, in actions which are not subject to privative jurisdiction, the sheriff may, on the motion of any of the parties to the cause, if he is of the opinion that the importance or difficulty of the cause make it appropriate to do so, remit the cause to the Court of Session. In any action for divorce or in an action in relation to the custody or adoption of a child, the sheriff may, of his own accord, remit the action to the Court of Session (Sheriff Courts (Scotland) Act 1971, s 37). If, in any proceedings against the Crown, a certificate by the Lord Advocate is produced to the effect that the proceedings may involve an important question of law, or may be decisive of other cases, or are for other reasons more fit for trial in the Court of Session, the sheriff must remit the proceedings to the Court of Session (Crown Proceedings Act 1947 s 44).

Within four days after the sheriff had pronounced an interlocutor remitting the cause to the Court of Session, the sheriff clerk must transmit the process to the deputy principal clerk of session, having, within the same period, sent written notice of the remit to the parties and certified on the interlocutor sheets that he has done so.

3. Remit of cause from the Court of Session (r 20A)

The Court of Session may, in relation to an action before it which could competently have been brought before a sheriff, remit the action (at its own instance or on the application of any of the parties to the action) to the sheriff within whose jurisdiction the action could have been brought if, in the opinion of the court, the nature of the action makes it appropriate to do so (Law Reform (Miscellaneous Provisions) (Scotland) Act 1985 s 14).

When the process is received the sheriff clerk must note the date of receipt, enrol the cause on the first court day occurring not earlier than fourteen days after the date of receipt, and send notice of the date of calling to parties. The action then proceeds on the Court of Session process, unless the Sheriff otherwise directs.

Chapter 6

Undefended causes

1. Minute for granting decree without attendance (r 21)

As a general rule, if no notice of intention to defend has been lodged by the defender within the period of notice (see page 30), the pursuer's solicitor may endorse a minute on the initial writ asking the court to grant decree, without the need for the pursuer or his solicitor to appear in Court; this procedure is known as granting decree in absence. Exceptions to the general rule apply to actions:

    (i) of divorce or of separation;

    (ii) relating to custody, access, welfare or upbringing of chidren; and

    (iii) relating to parentage, legitimacy etc,

    for all of which see rr 22 and 23 below; or

    (iv) in causes in which the Hague Convention applies, in which case see r 21A below.

In practice the pursuer's solicitor checks with the sheriff clerk to find out if a notice of intention to defend or a minute under r 34 (see page 50) (if applicable) has been lodged by the defender. If not, the pursuer's solicitor endorses a minute on the initial writ craving decree and delivers the writ to the sheriff clerk. The procedure thereafter varies depending on the domicile of the defender.

(a) Defender domiciled in Scotland

If the sheriff is satisfied that:

    (i) no notice of intention to defend or minute under r 34 has been lodged;

    (ii) the defender is domiciled in Scotland and a ground of

jurisdiction exists under the Civil Jurisdiction and Judgments Act 1982 (the initial writ must contain averments to this effect - see r 3, page 26); and

(iii) the initial writ has been lawfully served and is accompanied by a certificate of citation,

decree is granted.

(b) Defender domiciled in another part of the United Kingdom or in another Contracting State

If the sheriff is satisfied that the requirements set out in *(a)* above have been met and, in addition, that the defender has been able to receive the initial writ in sufficient time to arrange for his defence or that all necessary steps have been taken to that end, decree is granted.

2. Decree in causes to which the Hague Convention applies (r 21A)

This rule deals with any civil proceedings (including proceedings for divorce, separation and actions for custody of children) in which the initial writ has been served in a country to which the *Hague Convention on the Service Abroad of Judicial Documents* applies. Before granting decree, the sheriff must be satisfied that, *inter alia*, the following requirements have been met:

(i) service has been effected in terms of r 12 (see above); or

(ii) service has been effected in a way which conforms to the following conditions:

- the document was transmitted by one of the methods provided for in the Convention;
- a period of not less than six months, as may be considered adequate by the sheriff, has elapsed since the date of transmission of the document; and
- no certificate of any kind has been received, even though every reasonable effort has been made to obtain it through the competent authorities of the State addressed.

3. Undefended actions relating to parental rights (r 22)

Rule 22 applies to actions relating to tutory, curatory, custody or access or any right or authority relating to the welfare or upbringing of a child conferred on a parent by any rule of law.

In an undefended action in which the pursuer craves decree, the initial writ is not presented to the sheriff in chambers but is enrolled by the sheriff clerk for calling in the ordinary court. Why this is necessary is not clear since it is unlikely that the defender would be present (there is no requirement to intimate the enrolment to any party).

The case having been called in court, the sheriff must be satisfied as to the proposed arrangements for the care and upbringing of any child and, if necessary, he will postpone his decision and call for a report on the circumstances, in terms of the Matrimonial Proceedings (Children) Act 1958 s 11.

See also r 23 below.

4. Procedure where actions of divorce or separation or actions affecting parentage are undefended (r 23)

Actions of divorce, actions of separation and actions for declarator of parentage, non-parentage, legitimacy, legitimation or illegitimacy can be classified as undefended in the following circumstances:
   (i)   where no notice of intention to defend has been lodged; or
   (ii) where the court has directed the action to proceed as undefended, including an action being defended otherwise than on the merits (see r 34, page 50)

Before granting decree in such actions, the sheriff has to be satisfied that the averments in the initial writ have been proved. The normal method of proof is by affidavit evidence (see r 72, page 71).

All Sheriffs Principal have issued written guidance on the form and content of affidavits. The directions are detailed and should be followed when affidavits are being drawn. The following points are worth noting:
   (i)   the rules (r 72) provide that "affidavit" includes affirmation and statutory or other declaration;
   (ii) the affidavit is admissible if emitted before a notary public or

any other competent authority - defined in the guidance as a Justice of the Peace, Commissioner of Oaths, or other statutory authority within the meaning of the Statutory Declarations Act 1835;

(iii) affirmations should follow the averments in the initial writ;

(iv) productions, such as photographs, should be docquetted and signed by the witness and person taking the affidavit;

(v) in cases involving custody of or access to children, the affidavit should present a full picture of the position regarding the child or children; and

(vi) where financial craves are involved the evidence should be full, accurate and up-to-date.

If the period of notice has expired and no notice of intention to defend, or minute under r 34 has been lodged, the pursuer's solicitor endorses a minute, in terms of Form X of the Rules, on the initial writ which, together with the affidavits, is lodged with the sheriff clerk.

The sheriff clerk checks that the procedural requirements have been met and passes the process to the sheriff for consideration.

If the sheriff is satisfied on all aspects of the case, he may grant decree. However, he may call for further information, for example if he is not satisfied with arrangements for the care of children, he may call for an independent report. If he feels that the affidavit evidence is inadequate, he may call for further evidence by affidavit or direct that the witnesses attend court to give parole (oral) evidence.

The sheriff clerk, on the expiry of 14 days after the grant of decree, issues to each party an extract of the decree (see page 47).

5. Decree for expenses (r 24)

It is normal when craving decree in absence to elect to charge the scale fee of expenses, and decree in terms of the crave and decree for expenses are granted together. However, if the pursuer elects to have expenses in the cause taxed by the auditor of court, decree for expenses will be granted at a later stage, ie when the auditor of court's report has been lodged and approved.

6. Issue of an extract decree (r 25)

The extract of a decree is the written authority for implementation of a decree or order of court. The extract may be issued by the sheriff clerk after the expiry of fourteen days from the date of decree. Apart from actions of divorce, in which issue of an extract decree is automatic, issue of an extract in undefended actions depends on a request by the pursuer's solicitor, usually made when the initial writ is returned for the grant of decree.

The sheriff, on cause shown, (for example that implementation of the decree may depend on action being taken very quickly), may order the issue of an extract at an earlier date.

7. Finality of decree in absence (r 26)

A decree in absence may be challenged in several ways:
  (i)   by reponing (see below);
  (ii) by raising an action, in the Court of Session, to have the decree reduced (set aside); or
  (iii) by raising an action, in the Court of Session, to have the decree suspended - the effect being that the execution of diligence on the decree is suspended until questions on the legal position have been determined.

In the absence of any challenge, the decree in absence becomes final and entitled to the privileges of a decree *in foro* (as in a case in which the defender has entered appearance) within six months of its date or the date of charge under it, provided that service of the initial writ or charge has been personal. In all other cases the decree in absence becomes final after twenty years from its date.

Section 9(7) of the Land Tenure Reform (Scotland) Act 1974 makes separate provisions for the finality of a decree granted under that Act.

8. Amendment of initial writ (r 27)

In an undefended action, the sheriff has the same power to allow amendment of the initial writ as he has in defended actions. The extent of the power is set out in r 64 (see page 66).

The need to request amendment normally arises after the initial writ has been served - and a defect has been identified in the designation of one or other of the parties, in which case the sheriff will normally allow amendment and order re-service of the writ. However, if the requested amendment is radical, eg substitution of one defender for another, the remedy may be to draw a new initial writ.

The defender will not be liable for expenses occasioned by the amendment, unless the sheriff otherwise directs.

If diligence, such as an arrestment on the dependence of the action (see Chapter 19), has been used before amendment of the initial writ, the amendment shall not have the effect of validating the diligence if this prejudices the rights of creditors of the debtor (who may be interested in defeating the diligence). But the amendment has the effect of obviating any objection by the defender, or any person representing him by a title, or in right of a debt contracted by him, subsequent to the execution of such diligence.

9. Reponing (r 28)

Reponing is a form of appeal. It applies to all decrees in absence in ordinary actions with the exception of actions for divorce and of separation.

A reponing note may be lodged at any time before implementation in full of a decree in absence. Implementation in full depends on the circumstances. If the decree has been complied with, eg by payment to the pursuer of the sum decerned for, reponing is not appropriate but where only part of the sum decerned for has been paid, the defender can be reponed for the balance.

The defender lodges with the sheriff clerk a note setting out his proposed defence to the action and his explanation for his failure to enter appearance. A copy of the note must be served on the pursuer. The normal practice is to serve a copy notice, by post or by hand, on the pursuer's solicitor before the note is lodged with the sheriff clerk. A diet is then fixed for hearing the application. The diet is intimated by the defender to the pursuer.

(a)   Consignation and recall of decree (r 29)

The defender must consign the sum of £10 with the sheriff clerk, in addition to court dues, when the note is lodged.

The application is considered at the hearing fixed and normal practice is to allow the pursuer to be heard, if he so wishes. If the sheriff is satisfied with the defender's explanation, he may recall the decree, so far as not implemented, and the action then goes ahead as if the defender had entered appearance.

(b)   Sist of diligence (r 30)

A reponing note, duly lodged and served on the pursuer operates as a sist of diligence - the execution of diligence is suspended but diligence already executed is not recalled.

(c)   Consigned money and expenses (r 31)

Whether or not the application is granted, the pursuer is entitled to uplift the consigned money, unless the sheriff otherwise directs, and the sheriff may make such order on expenses as seems just.

(d)   Judgment to be final (r 32)

The sheriff's decision recalling, or incidental to the recall of, a decree in absence is final and not subject to review, but a decision to refuse a reponing note is appealable to the Sheriff Principal or to the Court of Session (ss 27 and 28 of the 1907 Act).

Chapter 7

Defence

1. Notice of intention (r 33)

The warrant of citation attached to the service copy initial writ invites the defender, if he intends to defend the action, to lodge a notice of his intention with the sheriff clerk. The notice, in terms of Form F in the schedule to the rules, must be accompanied by the service copy initial writ and must be lodged before the period of notice has expired. The reason for requiring the service copy initial writ to be produced is to enable the sheriff clerk to calculate the expiry date of the period of notice (see page 30).

Failure to lodge the notice before the expiry of the period of notice might not be fatal. The defender could apply to the sheriff for an extension of the period by the exercise of the dispensing powers of the sheriff under r 1 (see page 39).

Lodging a notice of intention to defend covers not only defence of the action on its merits but also a challenge of the jurisdiction of the court; it does not imply acceptance of the jurisdiction of the court.

2. Minute relating to aliment, periodical allowance, capital payment and transfer of property (r 34)

This rule, which applies to specific actions, enables a defender who does not wish to defend an action on the merits, to apply to the court for an order relating to matters ancillary to the crave, for example to award an amount of aliment which is lower than that craved. It also provides for decree being granted in respect of matters not craved in the initial writ but which are agreed by parties in a joint minute. A notice of intention to defend is unnecessary. See also r 56 (page 61).

Where:
  (i)   in an action:
         •   of separation;
         •   of affiliation and aliment; or
         •   for the custody of children,
        a defender intends only to dispute the amount of aliment; or
  (ii) in an action of divorce, a defender intends only to dispute liability for, or the amount of, or raise other matters relating to:
         •   aliment;
         •   periodical allowance;
         •   capital payment; or
         •   transfer of property,
he may, in place of lodging a notice of intention to defend, lodge a minute condescending on the relevant facts.

In an action of divorce or separation the defender may, without lodging a notice of intention to defend, apply by minute, condescending on the relevant facts, for an order for aliment, periodical allowance, capital payment or transfer of property.

On a minute being lodged, the sheriff clerk fixes a date for a hearing and the defender must send a copy of the minute, and intimate the date of hearing, to the pursuer. The pursuer must then return the initial writ to the sheriff clerk at or before the hearing. No process need be made up unless the sheriff so directs. The sheriff may deal with the case as he thinks fit.

In the actions referred to above, decree may be granted in terms of a joint minute dealing with:
         •   aliment;
         •   periodical allowance;
         •   capital payment; or
         •   transfer of property,
whether or not these have been craved in the initial writ or a minute lodged in terms of this rule.

3. Tabling (r 35)

Tabling is a formal step in ordinary cause procedure in the sheriff court. The procedure applies to cases in which a notice of intention to defend has been lodged within the period of notice. The pursuer attends court and states "cause tabled".

The pursuer will be aware that a notice of intention has been lodged, either from his own enquiry or, in some courts, on the advice of the sheriff clerk who enrols the cause for tabling on the first designated ordinary court day occurring after expiry of the period of notice (see also 5 below).

If the cause has not been formally tabled and the defender has not craved protestation (see r 36 below), the cause is dropped from the roll without any order being made. The pursuer has three months in which to ask the sheriff to direct that the cause be again enrolled for tabling subject to intimation being made on the defender, re-service if appropriate, an award of expenses or any other order which the sheriff may make.

The normal first order is for the defender to lodge defences (see r 43 below). However, the sheriff may simply continue the cause to another date without an order, eg because there is a possibility of a settlement.

4. Protestation (r 36)

Protestation is a safeguard for the defender against a pursuer who raises an action and does no more. This could be particularly oppressive if the pursuer has arrested, on the dependence of the action, moveable property belonging to the defender.

The defender, having attended court on the day fixed for tabling and the pursuer not having tabled the cause, the defender produces the service copy initial writ and craves protestation. The sheriff, having considered the circumstances, may grant protestation and if he does so, he must make an order against the pursuer for payment to the defender of protestation money - no amount is specified in the rules.

Protestation by the defender is not restricted to the first tabling date. If the defender has not craved protestation at that time, he may, within three months of the first tabling date, ask the sheriff to direct that the cause be enrolled for tabling (as in r 35 above) so that he can then crave protestation if the cause is not tabled.

An extract of the award of protestation can be issued after the expiry of seven days from the date of its granting but in cases where arrestments have been used, as mentioned above, an extract can be issued after 48 hours.

The effect of protestation being extracted is that the instance falls, ie the case is at an end. However, this can be prevented if, before extract, the pursuer applies for recall of the protestation. If this is granted, the sheriff allows the cause to proceed, on payment of protestation money, and on such conditions as the sheriff thinks fit.

5. Lodging of process by pursuer

There is an onus on the pursuer to check with the sheriff clerk to find out if a notice of intention to defend has been lodged. If a notice has been lodged, the pursuer will be advised of the date on which the cause will be enrolled for tabling.

(a)   Preparation of process

The pursuer must then prepare a process consisting of:
    (i)   the principal initial writ;
    (ii) a copy initial writ with a warrant certifying it a true copy;
    (iii) principal interlocutor sheets;
    (iv) duplicate interlocutor sheets;
    (v) principal inventory of process; and
    (vi) borrowing inventory of process.

The sheriff clerk marks the date of lodging on all items of process.

(b)   Custody of process

Three items of process, the principal initial writ, the principal interlocutor sheets and the borrowing inventory of process remain in the custody of the sheriff clerk except that the sheriff may make a special order for the release of the principal initial writ.

(c)   Borrowing of process (r 39)

Solicitors in the action may wish to examine the process, for example to adjust their pleadings (see r 46 below). They can do so by visiting the sheriff clerk's office but, as a matter of convenience, they may borrow the process and work on it in their office. The process may be borrowed by the solicitor's authorised clerk, for whom the solicitor is responsible.

A party litigant cannot borrow a process except with leave of the sheriff subject to such conditions as the sheriff may impose. However, the party litigant is entitled to inspect the process in the sheriff clerk's office and, if practicable, be supplied with copies of parts of the process.

A solicitor, having borrowed a process, is under an obligation to return it to the court within a reasonable time. If he delays and the other side is being denied access to the process, the sheriff clerk will ask him to return the process. If this is not effective, other remedies, such as process caption which could lead to imprisonment of the solicitor or his clerk, are technically available, although such remedies are unknown in practice.

Where a proof has been fixed, any parts of the process which have been borrowed must be returned not later than two days before the proof. This is to give the sheriff an opportunity to read the pleadings, examine productions etc before the start of the proof.

(d)   Failure to return process (r 40)

The process must be present in court whenever the case is on the roll, so that it can be examined if necessary. Any one who borrows a process or part of a process must return it in time for any calling at which it is required. Failure to do so renders that person liable to a fine not exceeding £50, payable to the sheriff clerk. The order imposing the fine may be recalled by the sheriff who granted it, on cause shown. There is no appeal against the sheriff's order.

(e)   Replacement of lost documents (r 41)

A copy of any item of process which has been lost or destroyed can be treated as if it were the original, provided the copy is authenticated as directed by the sheriff.

(f)   Borrowing of certified copy initial writ for the purpose of arrestment (r 42)

The purpose of arrestment on the dependence of an action is to prevent the defender from disposing of part or all of his moveable property with the intention of preventing the pursuer from gaining access to the property in the event of a decree being granted in favour of the pursuer.

It is standard practice to include a crave for a warrant to arrest on the dependence in an initial writ which contains a pecuniary conclusion (other than expenses) and the warrant is included in the warrant to cite (Form B1). Arrestment is normally executed before tabling. If the pursuer wishes to arrest after tabling, when he will not have possession of the initial writ as authority for arresting, he may use the certified copy initial writ (which is borrowable) as authority.

A pursuer who wishes to arrest on the dependence, but has omitted to crave a warrant to arrest, may present the initial writ to the sheriff clerk for a document known as a precept of arrestment to be issued. This procedure is also available for execution of an arrestment on a liquid document of debt, for example a bill, but precepts of arrestment are rare or unknown in practice.

6. Defences (r 43)

The defender may lodge his written defences to the action at tabling. However, the normal practice is to await the order, made by the sheriff at tabling, for defences to be lodged within a specified period, usually seven days.

The case may be continued from the tabling date without an order for defences (see r 35, page 52). There are various reasons for this, for example the defender may require time to apply for legal aid or there may be a possibility of settlement and no need to lodge defences. However, if there is no such reason, the sheriff orders defences to be lodged so that the case may proceed.

At the time defences are lodged with the sheriff clerk, the defender must send a copy to the pursuer.

(a) Form of defences (r 44)

Just as the initial writ sets out the case for the pursuer, the written case for the defender is set out in the defences. The condescendence in the initial writ is in numbered paragraphs and the defences must be in the form of answers in corresponding paragraphs and, like the pursuer, the defender must append pleas-in-law. The result is that, by comparing one document with the other, it is possible to see the case for both parties.

In addition to written defences, the defender may lodge a counterclaim (see r 51, page 59).

(b) Implied admissions (r 45)

Defences, when first lodged, must contain answers to the pursuer's condescendence but they may, and normally do, introduce new matter. This in turn must be answered by the pursuer who, in answering, may raise new matter which requires answer by the defender and so on. If a statement of fact made by one party is within the knowledge of the other party and not specifically denied by that other party, the latter is held as admitting the fact. As a precaution, answers to the other side's statements often contain the phrase "not known and not admitted".

(c) Adjustment of pleadings (r 46)

The process by which each side answers the other's statements is known as adjustment of pleadings. This is done in writing on, or by attaching typescript to, the certified copy initial writ in the case of the pursuer, or the defences in the case of the defender. Any adjustment done by one party must be immediately intimated to all other parties in the case.

(d) Open record (r 47)

Extensive adjustment of the pleadings can make it difficult to read them. A "clean" and easily read copy of all pleadings is lodged when adjustment has been completed and the record closed (see r 62, page 65). As an interim measure, to bring some order to the pleadings, the sheriff may, either if asked by any party or without being asked, order the pursuer to lodge a re-type of the pleadings, including all adjustments to date. A copy of the resulting document, known as the open record, has to be sent to all other parties.

Further adjustments, if any, are written on the open record (as in r 46, above).

(e)   Alteration of sum sued for (r 48)

Adjustment of the initial writ or defences is restricted to condescendence, answers and pleas-in-law. Alteration of the crave is classed as an amendment and requires the permission of the sheriff (see r 64, page 66). The exception to this rule applies to alteration of the sum sued for. This amendment, which must be made on the initial writ, the certified copy initial writ and the open record (if any) is competent in a case in which all other parties have lodged defences or answers, and the record has not been closed. The pursuer must intimate the amendment to all other parties.

7. Adjustment period (r 49)

The purpose of the adjustment period is to give each party an opportunity to answer the other's case. The sheriff fixes the date, normally at tabling, on which the case will be called on the adjustment roll (two weeks from tabling). The theory is that most adjustments will have been completed within that period but, if not, one continuation on the adjustment roll is allowed, on request and without need to show cause. Thereafter, if a further continuation is requested, cause must be shown.

Receipt of a note of adjustments shortly before a calling date on the adjustment roll is an example of what might be regarded as sufficient cause to grant more than one continuation, but the number of such continuations depends largely on the policy of the sheriff. The fact that parties to the action agree on the case being continued on the adjustment roll is not sufficient cause.

In considering whether parties have had sufficient time in which to adjust pleadings, the sheriff must take into account any additional time provided by the intervention of a court vacation between callings of the case.

Chapter 8

Third party notice and counterclaim

1. Third party procedure (r 50)

Third party procedure is appropriate if the defender claims that:

(i)   he has a right of contribution, relief or indemnity against a third party, such as the right of an insured person against an insurer; or

(ii) a third party, whom the pursuer is not bound to call as a defender, is liable with the defender to the pursuer in respect of the subject matter of the cause, for example where, in an action of reparation for personal injury, the defender claims that a third party was wholly or partly to blame.

The purpose of the procedure is to provide an opportunity for all related claims to be dealt with at the same time. It is solely a procedural mechanism to bring the third party into the action; the merits are dealt with separately.

Averments directed against the third party will normally be entered in the pleadings at the adjustment stage. They must be made prior to the closing of the record or they may be made at a later stage, at the discretion of the sheriff but, in any event, not later than the commencement of the hearing of the case on its merits.

The procedure is as follows:

(i)   the defender sets out in his defences, or in a separate statement of facts, the grounds for his claim that the third party is liable to him or should be made a party to the cause;

(ii) the defences or statement of facts should contain appropriate pleas-in-law;

(iii) the defender lodges a motion, which may include craves for a warrant for arrestment to found jurisdiction or a warrant to arrest on the dependence, asking the sheriff to authorise service of a third party notice;

(iv) the period of notice for the third party notice is fixed in the same way as that for service of an initial writ (see r 7, page 30);

(v) if the motion is granted, the third party becomes a third party to the cause and a date is fixed for further procedure;

(vi) the notice should be in terms of Form G of the schedule to the rules, amended if necessary to suit the circumstances;

(vii) service of the notice, which should be accompanied by copies of the initial writ, defences and closed record (if the record has been closed - see page 65) is made in the same way as service of an initial writ;

(viii)after service, a copy of the notice and a certificate of execution must be lodged in process;

(ix) if the third party decides to lodge answers, he must do so on or before the date fixed for further procedure; and

(x) thereafter, the case proceeds in the normal way and the third party being a party to the cause, the sheriff may grant decree, interlocutor or order against him in the same way as for any other party to the cause.

Third party procedure is not restricted to the defender. The third party himself or a pursuer faced with a counterclaim by a defender may also use the procedure.

2. Counterclaim (r 51)

There is no restriction of the grounds on which a counterclaim may be made, but in practice it will be related to the question in controversy between the parties. The defender has a choice between raising a separate action or lodging a counterclaim. If he decides on the latter, he must lodge in process a separate document headed "Counterclaim for the Defender" and send a copy to the pursuer.

(a)   Form of counterclaim (r 52)

A counterclaim is akin to a substantive action and, in form, it is similar to an initial writ. It must contain a crave or craves, a statement (condescendence) setting out the facts on which the counterclaim is based and a note of pleas-in-law which are necessary to support the counterclaim.

(b)   Warrant of counterclaim (r 53)

The warrants for diligence granted to the pursuer when an initial writ is lodged are also available to the defender in respect of his counterclaim. The defender adds to the crave the words "warrant for arrestment on the dependence applied for". The sheriff clerk adds "Grants warrant as craved" and signs and dates the warrant.

(c)   Disposal of counterclaim (r 54)

The sheriff has a wide discretion in dealing with a counterclaim. He may deal with it as if it had been stated in a substantive cause, for example the counterclaim may go to proof. The sheriff may regulate procedure as he thinks fit but it would be unusual to depart from the procedure set out in the rules. He may grant decree for the counterclaim in whole or in part, or for the difference between it and the sum claimed in the initial writ.

(d)   Abandonment (r 55)

The pursuer may abandon the cause (see r 58 below) and the defender may abandon his counterclaim. The pursuer may do so despite the fact that a counterclaim has been lodged, in which case the abandonment does not affect the counterclaim which proceeds as a cause in its own right.   Any expenses payable by the pursuer in respect of his abandonment of the cause are separate from expenses of the counterclaim.

A similar procedure applies where the defender decides to abandon his counterclaim. The defender lodges a minute of abandonment in the process, the sheriff orders payment by the defender of expenses incurred by the pursuer in connection with the counterclaim and, on payment of these expenses, the sheriff dismisses the counterclaim. Dismissal does not preclude the defender from raising the subject matter of the counterclaim at a later date. However, if the defender fails to pay the expenses within fourteen days of the taxation, the pursuer is entitled to ask for a decree of absolvitor with expenses and if that is granted, the defender is precluded from raising the subject matter at a later date.

(e)   Counterclaim for custody, access or maintenance (r 56)

The defender has the same rights as the pursuer to make a claim in actions in which custody of, access to, or maintenance for a child is sought. The procedure is identical with that for counterclaims described above.

The defender, rather than lodge a separate minute under r 34, may include in the counterclaim a crave for an order for:
- aliment;
- periodical allowance;
- capital payment; or
- transfer of property.

The sheriff may grant decree in terms of a joint minute for the orders referred to above and also for custody of, access to or maintenance for a child, whether or not these have been craved in the initial writ or counterclaim.

Chapter 9

Incidental procedure

1. Motions (r 57)

Any motion endorsed as unopposed may be granted by the sheriff in chambers without hearing the parties. The purpose of this rule is to avoid the expense of attendance at court by solicitors acting for either or both parties. The motion must be in writing and the consenting party need only write "unopposed" or "I consent" and sign the statement. It is used in various circumstances, for example for recall of a sist of procedure, or for an award of interim aliment.

The motion is granted subject to the discretion of the sheriff. He may call for further information, for example where the motion is for interim custody of a child, or he may direct the motion to be heard in court, eg if the motion is to discharge a diet of proof at a later date.

The procedure also covers joint minutes.

2. Abandonment of cause (r 58)

The pursuer may offer to abandon the cause at any time before decree of absolvitor or dismissal (both in favour of the defender) has been granted. The procedure is as follows:

(i) a minute by the pursuer offering to abandon the cause is lodged in process;

(ii) the sheriff finds the pursuer liable to the defender in expenses and remits an account of expenses to the auditor of court for taxation;

(iii) if the pursuer pays the defender the taxed amount of expenses within fourteen days of the taxation, the sheriff may dismiss the cause; and

(iv) if the pursuer does not pay the defender the expenses within fourteen days of the taxation, the defender may apply for a decree of absolvitor with expenses.

If a decree of dismissal has been granted, the action may be raised again; if the decree is one of absolvitor, the action may not be raised again.

3. Decree by default (r 59)

The progress of a defended ordinary action depends on action being taken by one side or the other or both. The exception to this is where procedure has been sisted, eg to allow the defender to apply for legal aid. If one side fails to take action required of him, the other side may be entitled to decree - known as decree by default. The circumstances in which a decree by default may be granted are:

(i) failure to lodge any production or pleading;

(ii) failure to implement an order of the sheriff within the time required; or

(iii) failure to appear or to be represented at a diet,

in which cases the sheriff may grant decree as craved, if the default has been by the defender, or decree of absolvitor or dismissal if the default has been by the pursuer, with expenses to the successful party. These decrees are at the discretion of the sheriff who may, on cause shown, extend the time for lodging any production or pleading or for implementing any order. So far as failure of a party to appear is concerned, the sheriff may continue the case to another diet and give the party an opportunity to appear or be represented.

If none of the parties appears at a diet, the sheriff may dismiss the cause. No decree is granted nor is there an award of expenses.

Decree by default procedure does not apply to actions of divorce or of separation, in which proof is required before decree can be granted.

4. Late appearance by defender in actions of divorce and of separation (r 59A)

As a rule, a notice of intention to defend must be lodged within the period of notice, failing which reponing (see page 48) may be the remedy. An exception to the rule applies to the defender in an action of divorce or of separation who may apply to the sheriff for leave to:

    (i)   appear and be heard at a diet of proof;

    (ii)   lodge defences and to lead evidence at any time before decree has been pronounced; or

    (iii) appeal within fourteen days of the date of decree.

The defender may not lead evidence without the consent of the pursuer and the pursuer is entitled to lead further evidence or to recall witnesses even if the pursuer has closed his case before leave is granted.

The sheriff, in granting leave, may impose such conditions as he thinks fit, for example that the pursuer be found entitled to expenses to the date of leave being granted.

5. Transfer of cause on death of party (r 60)

Where one of the parties to the cause has died and his representatives do not enter the cause, any party may lodge a minute craving transfer of the cause against the representatives.

If a minute craving transference is lodged, the sheriff may:

    (i)   grant warrant for service of the initial writ on the representatives;

    (ii)   allow them to lodge a minute of objections within a specified time; and

    (iii) order intimation to any other parties to the cause.

The sheriff, having considered any objections, may transfer the cause against the representatives.

6. Effect of absence of interlocutors (r 61)

Before this rule was made, an ordinary action was held to have fallen asleep if no interlocutor was pronounced within a year and a day of the date of the last interlocutor. An action which had fallen asleep required to be wakened by lodging a minute of wakening in process. The concept of falling asleep (and wakening) has been abolished, so that the absence of an interlocutor now has no effect.

Chapter 10

Closing of record to proof

1. Closing of the record (r 62)

Closing of the record is a significant event in ordinary action procedure. Adjustment of the pleadings has been completed and the action is entering the final stages leading to a decision.

When the sheriff has closed the record, there is an onus on the pursuer to lodge a certified copy of the closed record within fourteen days.

The closed record is a conjunction of the written pleadings of the pursuer and defender presented in such a form that the sheriff can read through the case for each party by perusing one document. The instance and crave of the initial writ are followed by the condescendence and answers in such a way that each article of condescendence is followed immediately by the answer for the defender. The pleas-in-law of the pursuer are followed by the pleas-in-law for the defender and finally, all interlocutors pronounced up to and including the one closing the record are shown.

Having closed the record, the sheriff makes such order as he thinks fit. Normally, this consists of an order fixing a diet of proof (a date on which the evidence of witnesses will be heard), or a diet of debate (at which each side will present a legal argument on preliminary pleas).

2. Preliminary pleas (r 63)

A preliminary plea is a plea-in-law, by the pursuer or defender, which, if sustained by the sheriff, would end the action. Preliminary pleas are normally directed against the competency of the action, for example the pursuer has no title to sue the defender; or the relevancy of the pleadings, for example the defences are irrelevant and lacking in specification.

Preliminary pleas are reviewed at closing of the record. Any preliminary plea which is not insisted on will be repelled by the sheriff at that time. Parties must state the preliminary pleas, if any, on which they insist and the sheriff will fix a diet of debate on the pleas. If either party considers that a preliminary plea requires evidence to be led before the sheriff reaches a decision on it, he may ask the sheriff to allow a proof before answer.

The sheriff may sustain or repel a preliminary plea. If the plea is to the competency and is sustained, the action will be dismissed, normally with expenses to the defender. A plea to relevancy, if sustained, will generally lead to decree with expenses to the successful party, unless the sheriff grants leave to amend the pleadings. Repel of preliminary pleas leaves the way clear for the action to go to proof.

3. Amendment of pleadings (r 64)

The sheriff has power to allow amendment of the pleadings at any time before final judgment, his main consideration being to ensure that the issue between the parties is in sharp focus. With the exception of the amendment of the amount sued for, which may be done without leave before the record is closed (see r 48, page 57), all amendments require the leave of the sheriff.

The following amendments may be made:
- (i) any defect in the designation of parties may be corrected;
- (ii) an additional or substitute pursuer may be added to the cause;
- (iii) an additional or substitute defender and averments against him may be added. If a motion to do so is granted, the initial writ, defences and closed record (if any), as amended, are served on the new defender with a notice in terms of Form H to the Rules. A copy of the notice and a certificate of execution must be lodged in process;
- (iv) the condescendence, defences, answers and pleas in law may be amended as far as is necessary to determine the real question in controversy.

In allowing amendments, the sheriff may attach whatever conditions he considers necessary and it is normal to make an award of expenses against the party making the amendment.

No amendment prejudices the rights of creditors of the defender by giving validity to diligence used on dependence of the cause; but no objection shall be effective when stated by the defender, or any person representing him, subsequent to the execution of such diligence.

4. Renouncing of probation (r 65)

Following the closing of the record, it is normal to fix a proof or, if there are preliminary pleas, a debate. However, if the parties are agreed that the action does not raise questions of fact but only law, they may forego the right to a proof and lodge a joint minute to that effect with the sheriff clerk, with or without a statement of admitted facts and productions, and the sheriff, if satisfied that it is right to do so, will order the case to be debated.

5. Ordering of proof (r 66)

If proof is necessary, as for example where the case has neither been sent for nor decided in debate, the sheriff fixes a date for proof to be led.

There are various modes of proof depending on the circumstances:

(a) Proof at large

This is the most common mode. The sheriff allows to parties a proof of their respective averments, parole (oral) evidence is led by the examination of witnesses, the solicitors acting for parties address the sheriff on the evidence and a judgment is issued by the sheriff.

(b) Proof habili modo

While most proofs consist of parole evidence, it may be that part of a case can only be proved by writ, in which case, the motion to fix a proof should be for a proof *habili modo*. This leaves it to the discretion of the sheriff to decide on the type of evidence to be led.

In addition to specifying the mode of proof, the sheriff may limit the proof, eg by excluding proof of averments which are irrelevant, by restricting proof of specified averments to the writ or oath of the defender (see r 67, below). The limitation should be contained in the interlocutor ordering the proof.

6. Reference to oath (r 67)

Reference to oath is rare, if not unknown, in practice. Its main use is in cases in which it is the only means of proof, for example to establish a loan in the absence of writing. The oath of the deponent takes the place of a proof.

Application for a reference is made after the record has been closed and preliminary pleas disposed of, and takes the form of a minute lodged with the sheriff clerk. The minute may be signed by the party making the reference or by his solicitor, in which case the solicitor should have written authority to apply for the reference. The sheriff may grant the reference (and attach whatever conditions he thinks fit) or refuse it.

If the party to whose oath reference has been made fails to appear at the diet, the sheriff may hold him as confessed and grant decree.

7. Objections to documents (r 68)

Normally a challenge of a deed or writing, such as to its validity, requires an action of reduction to be raised. Such an action is incompetent in the sheriff court and must be raised in the Court of Session. Objections to a deed or writing founded on by any party in an ordinary action may be taken by way of exception without the need to raise an action of reduction. Where such an objection is taken, and an action of reduction would be competent, the sheriff may order the objector to find caution or to make consignation.

8. Remit to person of skill (r 69)

When an action is concerned with technical matters, such as building construction, accounting or repairs to machinery, it may be preferable to have a person who is well acquainted with the technicalities to examine the matter and report back to the court. The procedure is known as a remit to a person of skill and is designed to render unnecessary proof of the matter dealt with by the reporter. Lists of persons qualified and willing to act as reporters are maintained by most professional and trade associations. Both parties must agree to the remit, which may be made before or after closing of the record. The procedure is:

(i) parties must lodge a joint minute setting out:
- the matters which are to be the subject of the remit;
- the name and designation of a reporter who is qualified and willing to act - provided that this has also been agreed;

(ii) the sheriff has a discretion on whether or not to remit. If parties are not agreed on the reporter, the sheriff will nominate one;

(iii) the expense of the execution of the remit is borne by the parties equally unless the sheriff otherwise directs;

(iv) the report is final and conclusive on the matter remitted, but parties are entitled to be heard on the report before it is adopted by the sheriff;

(v) a remit may be made in an undefended case, on the motion of the pursuer.

Chapter 11

Evidence, witnesses and havers

1. Evidence to lie *in retentis* (r 70)

Evidence which is in danger of being lost, for example because a witness is seriously ill or has to go abroad, may be taken before the main proof. The sheriff may grant a motion by either party to take the evidence and the motion may be made at any time after the action has been raised. The sheriff may take the evidence himself or appoint a commissioner to do so.

The evidence having been taken down, it lies *in retentis* until the case goes to proof, at which stage the sheriff decides whether or not it should be received as evidence in the case.

The motion should state:
    (i)   the reason for the request;
    (ii) the name of the witness to be examined; and
    (iii) if the witness is able to attend court.

If, for reasons of ill health, the witness cannot attend court, a medical certificate to that effect should be lodged. In such cases, the sheriff or commissioner will attend on the witness. If the witness can attend court, he should be cited in the usual manner (see r 75, page 74).

The evidence is recorded in the same way as at proof (see r 73, page 72).

2. Evidence taken on commission (r 71)

The evidence of any witness or haver (person having an article required for the proof):

(i)   resident beyond the jurisdiction of the court;

(ii) who, although resident within the jurisdiction resides at some place remote from the court; or

(iii) who, by reason of illness, age or infirmity or other sufficient cause, is unable to attend the diet of proof,

may be taken by a commissioner in the same manner as evidence to lie *in retentis* (see r 70 above).

Evidence taken on commission is part of the proof in the cause and, unlike evidence to lie *in retentis*, it is received into process without further hearing.

The evidence is recorded in the manner set out in r 73; see below.

A witness over the age of seventy cannot be compelled to attend court but may have his evidence taken on commission.

The procedure for taking the evidence of a witness resident abroad is set out in the Codifying Act of Sederunt Book L Chapter II.

3. Affidavit evidence (r 72)

Affidavit evidence, as opposed to parole evidence, is admissible in:

(i)   actions of divorce, of separation, and of declarator of parentage, non-parentage, legitimacy, legitimation or illegitimacy which proceed as undefended; and

(ii) opposed interim orders under the Matrimonial Homes (Family Protection) (Scotland) Act 1981.

Separate provisions apply to actions mentioned at (i) above in which it appears to the sheriff that a defender is suffering from a mental disorder within the meaning of the Mental Health (Scotland) Act 1984. Affidavit evidence is admissible in such actions only if the curator *ad litem* for the defender has lodged a minute intimating that he does not intend to defend the action.

"Affidavit" includes affirmation and statutory or other declaration.

Practice Notes issued by Sheriffs Principal give detailed guidance on the preparation and content of affidavits. The practice note for the sheriffdom should be consulted before lodging affidavits in a sheriff court in that sheriffdom.

An affidavit is admissible if emitted before:
- a Notary Public;
- a Justice of the Peace;
- a Commissioner of Oaths; or
- a statutory authority within the meaning of the Statutory Declarations Act 1835.

A written statement by a qualified medical practitioner, and signed by him, is admissible in place of parole evidence.

Affidavits may be lodged after the expiry of the period within which a notice of intention to defend or a minute under r 34 must be lodged (see page 50). They should be accompanied by the initial writ with a minute in terms of Form X to the rules endorsed thereon.

The sheriff considers the whole cause, and without requiring the pursuer to attend, may grant decree or other order in terms of the minute. However, the sheriff may decide not to grant decree or such other order and, instead, remit the cause for such other procedure, including parole evidence, as he may deem appropriate (see r 23, page 45).

4. Recording of evidence (r 73)

The evidence led in the proof in all defended ordinary causes is recorded in shorthand unless all parties, with the consent of the sheriff, agree to dispensing with the recording of evidence - an unusual, if not unknown, practice.

Evidence taken on commission (see r 71 above) may be recorded by a shorthand writer or by a clerk approved by the commissioner.

Responsibility for instructing a shorthand writer in a proof or in a commission rests with the pursuer or the party moving the commission respectively.

Before recording the evidence, the shorthand writer or clerk is put under oath to correctly record the evidence which is recorded in the form of question and answer.

When the proof has been completed, the shorthand writer extends the notes of evidence and certifies them as a correct record. If the correctness of the extended notes or a deposition is challenged, the sheriff may take whatever action is necessary, including the recall of witnesses, to satisfy himself on the correctness of the notes, and he may amend the record of evidence as necessary.

Payment of the shorthand writer's fees is the responsibility of the person moving for the commission or, in the case of a proof, by the parties equally and the solicitors of parties are personally liable for making payment.

The above procedure applies to defended causes. It is unnecessary to record evidence in an undefended proof.

5. Witnesses and havers

(a) Citation (r 74)

When a proof or any other hearing in the cause requires the attendance of witnesses or havers (a haver is a person having custody of a document which is or is thought to be relevant to the cause), the fact that proof has been allowed or a diet for a hearing has been fixed by the sheriff is normally sufficient authority for the citation of witnesses and havers. If, for any reason, the authority to cite is challenged or if it is anticipated that it will be challenged, a copy of the interlocutor allowing the proof or fixing the diet, certified by the sheriff clerk, should be obtained.

A witness or haver must be given at least seven days' notice to attend a diet. He is advised in the citation that he may ask for travelling expenses to be paid to him in advance. If he has been given sufficient notice and travelling expenses, if any were requested, and fails to attend the diet, he will be liable to a penalty, not exceeding £250, unless the sheriff was satisfied that there was reasonable excuse for the failure. Any penalty is payable to the party on whose behalf the witness or haver was cited and a decree will be granted for its recovery.

(b) Form and service of citation (r 75)

Witnesses and havers are cited in terms of Form I in the schedule to the rules and the certificate of citation should be in terms of Form J.

Citations are normally sent by post (recorded delivery service) by a solicitor. If this method fails, a sheriff officer may be instructed to effect service. A solicitor who cites a witness or haver is personally liable for the fees and expenses of the witness or haver. If service is by sheriff officer the party citing the witness or haver is liable.

If a solicitor, having cited a witness or haver, intimates to the witness or haver that the citation has been cancelled, he must advise the witness that the cancellation does not affect any other citation the witness or haver may have received from another party in the cause.

(c) Second diligence against witnesses (r 76)

If it is anticipated that a witness or haver will fail to attend a diet of court, for example because a postal citation has been returned marked "Refused", the party citing the witness or haver may produce a valid certificate of citation and apply for letters of second diligence which, if granted, authorise an officer of court to arrest the witness or haver. The letters also authorise the officer of court to imprison the witness or haver, but the normal procedure is to bring him before the bar of the court when the sheriff may decide to imprison him or order him to attend a further diet of court, with or without finding caution for his appearance.

Decree for the expenses of the application may be granted against the witness or haver; these would be in addition to any penalty imposed under r 74.

(d) Warrant to arrest (r 77)

If, at the time of proof or hearing, a witness or haver fails to attend, having been duly cited, the sheriff, on the motion of the party who cited the witness or haver, and on production of a valid certificate of citation, may grant warrant for the apprehension, by an officer of court, of the witness or haver and for bringing him to the court.

There is a possibility that, if the witness or haver is apprehended on the day of the proof or hearing, he can be brought before the court on that day and his evidence taken.

Decree for the expenses may be awarded against the witness or haver; these would be in addition to any penalty imposed under r 74.

Chapter 12

Productions and proof

1. Introduction

All parties to the cause are expected to lodge documents or other productions which are founded on in the pleadings or which are relevant to the cause. If any party, having been lawfully required to do so, fails to lodge a document which is in his custody or power, the sheriff may order production of the document or appoint a commissioner to make enquiry, recover documents, if necessary, and report back to him. The latter procedure, which is known as granting a commission and diligence, can be a lengthy and expensive one. An optional (and shorter) procedure is available; see r 81, page 77.

Special provisions apply to the production of public records and bankers' books.

2. Production and recovery of documents (r 78)

Each party to the cause must lodge any document which is:
  (i) founded on in pleadings; and
  (ii) in his custody or power
along with the pleadings or before the record is closed, if required to do so by any other party to the cause or the sheriff.

If the documents, having been ordered to be produced, are not produced or are in the hands of a third party, the sheriff may, on the motion of any party, grant commission and diligence for recovery of the documents and may delay closing the record. However, if the documents are in the custody or power of a party and he fails to produce them, having been ordered to do so, the sheriff, on being so moved, may grant decree by default (see r 59, above).

The above procedures apply to documents which are founded on in the pleadings. At any time after tabling, the sheriff may grant commission and diligence for recovery of such documents contained in a specification, as the sheriff considers are relevant to the cause.

3. Lodging productions for proof (r 79)

Apart from documents which are requested or ordered to be produced (see r 78 above), all documents and other productions must be lodged, with an inventory, on or before the fourteenth day before the date fixed for proof. At the same time, notice of the lodging must be sent to all other parties in the cause.

If any party wishes to lodge any document or other production after the above date, he must have either the consent of the other parties or the permission of the sheriff, who may make an order on expenses or otherwise as seems just.

The productions, having been lodged, may be borrowed but must be returned not later than two days before the proof (see r 9, page 31)

4. Ordering of production of documents by the sheriff (r 80)

The sheriff has wide powers to order production of documents and may do so at any stage. He may allow any party, at any time before judgment, to produce any document which has not been produced in time. The sheriff may make an order on expenses and, if he considers it necessary, allow further proof.

5. Optional procedure before executing commission and diligence (r 81)

Any party to the cause may apply to the sheriff for a commission and diligence for the recovery of documents from any other party to the cause or from a haver. Application for a commission and diligence is accompanied by a specification of the documents to be recovered. The sheriff decides which documents in the specification may be recovered by diligence.

It is open to the party who has obtained the commission and diligence to ask the sheriff to appoint a commissioner to execute diligence, or he may elect to use the following optional procedure:

(i) An order, with certificate attached, in terms of Form K in the schedule to the Rules is prepared;

(ii) the order is served, by registered or recorded delivery post, and may be posted to the solicitor acting for the party or haver from whom the documents are to be recovered;

(iii) the order includes a specification of the documents to be produced;

(iv) the person to whom the order is addressed is directed to lodge all documents in the specification which are in his possession, with the sheriff clerk, by hand or by registered or recorded delivery post, within seven days from service of the order;

(v) in addition to any documents in the specification, there must be lodged with the sheriff clerk:

- an inventory of the documents lodged;
- the original order; and
- a signed and completed certificate (see (vii) below);

(vi) if the possessor of the documents claims confidentiality, the documents must be lodged but may be placed in a sealed packet marked "confidential" - see also r 82, page 79.

(vii) the certificate should reflect whichever of the following circumstances applies:

- that the documents produced are all of the documents in the possession of the recipient of the order which are in the specification; or
- that the recipient has no documents in his possession which are in the specification; or
- that documents in the specification exist, but were last seen in the hands of a (named) person on a specific date; or
- that the recipient knows of no other person in possession of any documents in the specification.

When the order, certificate and inventoried documents (if any) have been received by the sheriff clerk, he sends notice to the solicitors of all parties to the cause that the order has been obtempered. The notice specifies which (if any) of the documents in the specification have been lodged.

The party who served the order has an exclusive right to borrow any of the documents for a period of seven days from the date of the official intimation. Thereafter the other parties to the cause may borrow the document.

The purpose of the optional procedure is to reduce expense. However, if the party who served the order is dissatisfied with the results, for example if he is of the view that full production has not been made or that adequate reason for non-production has not been given, he may revert to commission and diligence procedure.

If extracts from books are produced, the sheriff, on cause shown, may order that the party obtaining the commission be allowed to inspect the originals and take copies but if confidentiality is claimed, the sheriff may direct that inspection and copy-taking be carried out in the presence of the appointed commissioner. The sheriff may order the production of any books (except bankers' books or books of public record) notwithstanding the production of certified extracts.

6. Confidentiality (r 82)

If any party to the cause or a haver, having been required to produce a document, either under commission and diligence or the optional procedure, claims confidentiality for the document produced, the document must be enclosed in a sealed packet and marked "confidential". The packet cannot be opened, or put in process, unless the sheriff, on the application of the party who executed the commission and diligence or who served the order under the optional procedure, authorises it to be done, having first given the party or haver making production, the opportunity to be heard.

7. Warrant for production of original documents from public records (r 83)

Extracts from public records are normally acceptable as productions in an ordinary cause. If it is necessary to produce the original register or deed from either the Keeper of the Registers of Scotland or the Keeper of the Records of Scotland, the following procedure must be followed:

(i) the party wishing to obtain the register or deed should write to the Keeper in charge of the originals giving notice of his intention to request production;

(ii) not earlier than seven days after giving notice, a written motion should be lodged, specifying the registers or deeds to be produced;

(iii) if the sheriff is satisfied that it is necessary for the ends of justice that the motion should be granted, he signs an interlocutor, including specification of the registers and deeds and the date of the proof or hearing, to that effect;

(iv) the party should write to the Principal Clerk of Session, enclosing a copy of the Sheriff's interlocutor, duly certified by the sheriff clerk or one of the deputes, for an order from the Lords of Council and Session authorising the Keeper to exhibit the original register or deed to the sheriff;

(v) The Principal Clerk submits the application to a Lord Ordinary in Chambers and, if warrant is granted, a certified copy of the warrant is served on the Keeper;

(vi) the production is not given to the party. A member of the Keeper's staff will bring it to the proof or hearing for inspection and will thereafter return it to the Keeper; and

(vii) any expense incurred in the transmission and liabilities of the production falls to be defrayed in the first instance by the party making the application.

8. Orders for inspection (r 84)

It is to be expected that parties to the cause will have reasonable access to documents and other productions relevant to the cause. If any party encounters difficulty in gaining access to a production, the sheriff has power to make various orders to remedy matters, for example by ordering production of documents or by granting a commission and diligence for recovery of documents (see rr 78 and 80 above). These remedies apply to documents.

Any party to the cause may apply to the sheriff for an order for the inspection, photographing, preservation, custody or detention of documents or other property (including, where appropriate, land) or for the production, recovery or taking of samples or for carrying out experiments on the document or other property. The application may be made before or after the commencement of proceedings and the following procedure applies:

(a) *After proceedings have commenced:*
 (i) a minute specifying the order sought and craving the sheriff to grant the order is lodged;
 (ii) a diet is fixed for a hearing on the application and intimation is ordered on the parties to the cause and such other persons as appear to the sheriff to have a relevant interest, eg the person in possession of the article to be inspected;
 (iii) the sheriff, after hearing the parties, may grant or refuse the application in whole or in part;
 (iv) the sheriff may order the applicant to find caution for any loss, damage or expenses incurred as a result of the application; and
 (v) the person obtaining an order must send a certified copy of the interlocutor granting the order to any party to the cause who was not present or represented when the application was heard and also to any other person to whom the sheriff appoints intimation to be made.

(b) *Before proceedings have commenced*
 (i) a summary application, in the form of an initial writ, may be lodged by any person who appears to the sheriff to be likely to be a party or minuter in proceedings to be brought;
 (ii) a diet is fixed for a hearing and there is an order for service of the initial writ on all persons who are likely to be parties to the action when it is commenced and such other persons as appear to the sheriff to have a relevant interest;
 (iii) the sheriff may order the applicant to find caution for any loss, damage or expenses incurred as a result of the application;
 (iv) the person obtaining an order must send a certified copy of the interlocutor granting the order to any person on whom service of the initial writ was ordered, but who was not present or represented when the application was heard and also to any other person to whom the sheriff appoints intimation to be made.

9. Orders to disclose identity of persons (r 84A)

Application may be made to the sheriff for an order directing a person to disclose information as to the identity of other persons where identity cannot be established by other means. Procedure differs depending on whether the application relates to a current action or in a further action.

(a) Current action

Application for an order requiring a person to disclose any information he has as to the identity of a person who might be a witness in the cause is made by minute in the process. A diet is fixed, the minute is intimated to any other party to the cause and any other person who appears to have an interest. After hearing parties, the sheriff grants or refuses the order subject to such conditions as he thinks fit.

(b) Future action

Application for an order requiring a person to disclose any information he has on the identity of a person who might be a witness or a defender in proceedings which are likely to be brought is made by a summary application. The sheriff may order intimation on such persons as appear to him to have an interest. After hearing parties, the sheriff grants or refuses the order subject to such conditions as he thinks fit.

In both the above types of application, a certified copy interlocutor granting an order must be:
(i) served on the person to whom it is directed; and
(ii) intimated to any person who received intimation of the minute or the application, as the case may be
by the party in whose favour it has been granted, unless any of the persons referred to was present or represented when the application was determined.

10. Procedure at proof

(a) Proof to be taken continuously (r 85)

Proof should be taken continuously, ie day by day but the sheriff may adjourn the diet from time to time, for example because a witness is unavailable.

(b) Objections (r 86)

The procedure for recording objections depends on whether or not a shorthand writer has been appointed. If a shorthand writer has been appointed to record evidence:
  (i)   at a proof;
  (ii) to lie *in retentis;*
  (iii) taken by a commissioner; or
  (iv) at the execution of a commission and diligence for the recovery of documents,
any objection to the admissibility of oral or documentary evidence, to the production of documents, or the submissions of parties in relation to the decision of the sheriff or commissioner on the objections, must be recorded by the shorthand writer, if considered necessary or desirable at the discretion of the sheriff or commissioner.

If the services of a shorthand writer have been dispensed with (see r 73 above) the sheriff, if called on to do so, must:
  (i)   record in a separate note, the terms of objections to the admissibility of evidence on the grounds of confidentiality or to the production of a document on any ground and his decision thereon; and
  (ii) in all other cases record the terms of objections and his decision, in the note to the interlocutor disposing of the merits of the case.

Additionally, the sheriff or commissioner may, if he considers an objection of sufficient importance, direct that the evidence to which the objection relates should be recorded separately from the other evidence in the case.

(c) Incidental appeal against rulings on confidentiality and production of documents (r 87)

A party to the cause or other person (eg a witness or haver), who objects to the admissibility of oral or documentary evidence on the ground of confidentiality, or to producing a document on any ground, and is dissatisfied with the ruling of the sheriff may, with leave of the sheriff, appeal to the Sheriff Principal who must dispose of the appeal with the least possible delay. No other form of appeal against a decision of the sheriff on admissibility of evidence or production of documents is competent during the proof.

The sheriff may proceed with the parts of the proof which are not dependent on the ruling appealed against.

An appeal against the decision of a commissioner requires leave of the sheriff.

(d) Parties to be heard at close of proof (r 88)

The hearing on evidence may proceed immediately after the close of proof whether or not the evidence has been recorded by a shorthand writer. In complicated cases it might be considered desirable to have the shorthand notes extended in which case the hearing takes place at a later date.

Having heard parties or their procurators on the evidence, the sheriff may pronounce judgment there and then or he may make avizandum (reserve judgment).

Chapter 13

Judgment

1. Final judgment (r 89)

A final judgment on the merits of an ordinary cause consists of:
  (i) an interlocutor setting out:
       • findings in fact and in law separately;
       • the decree or order; and
       • a finding of liability for expenses, although these may
         not have been quantified;
  (ii) a note setting out the grounds on which the sheriff has
       proceeded.

The note is for the information of the parties to the cause and also for a
court dealing with any subsequent appeal. The requirement to write a
note applies to all interlocutors except those of a formal nature, but does
not apply to actions of divorce or of separation and aliment which
proceed as undefended.

Practice Notes operative in all sheriffdoms direct appellants, on marking
an appeal against an interlocutor, to request the sheriff to write a note if
none has been appended.

If an interlocutor with note appended is pronounced otherwise than in
the presence of parties (and, normally, it is so pronounced), a copy of
the interlocutor and note is sent by the sheriff clerk forthwith, and, free
of charge, to all parties to the cause.

The sheriff may sign an interlocutor outwith the sheriffdom but the date
of the interlocutor is the date on which it is entered in the books of
court.

Any clerical or incidental error may be corrected at any time prior to extract or before transmission of a process in which an appeal has been marked.

2. Extract (r 90)

Implementation of a decree, interlocutor or other order of court depends on the issue of an extract containing details of the decree or otherwise, and a warrant for the execution of diligence.

An extract of a decree in a defended cause may be issued after the expiry of fourteen days from the date of decree, unless:

(i)   an appeal has been marked; or
(ii) an application for leave to appeal has been marked; or
(iii) the sheriff has allowed extract to be applied for and issued earlier; or
(iv) the sheriff has reserved the question of expenses.

In the case of (iii) above, the motion for early extract must either be made in the presence of parties or the sheriff must be satisfied that written intimation of the motion has been given to all other parties.

In the case of (iv) above, extract may be issued after the expiry of fourteen days from the date of the interlocutor disposing of the question of expenses.

Apart from the above provisions, the sheriff has power to supersede extract until a date later than fourteen days from the date of decree.

The form and content of extracts is laid down in the schedule to the Sheriff Courts (Scotland) Extracts Act 1892.

Extracts of decrees of divorce should accord with Form Z in the schedule to the rules (r 90A).

Chapter 14

Appeal

The following modes of appeal are available in ordinary causes:
- (i)   from the sheriff to the Sheriff Principal;
- (ii) from the sheriff to the Court of Session; and
- (iii) from the Sheriff Principal to the Court of Session.

The mode will depend on the types of interlocutor against which the appeal is taken, and leave to appeal may be required.

1. Appeal to the Sheriff Principal

The following interlocutors may be appealed from the sheriff to the Sheriff Principal without leave:
- (i)   a final judgment, ie an interlocutor which, by itself, or taken along with other interlocutors, disposes of the subject matter of the cause, notwithstanding that judgment may not have been pronounced on every question raised, and that expenses found due may not have been modified, taxed or decerned for;
- (ii) an interlocutor granting or refusing interdict - interim or final;
- (iii) an interlocutor granting an interim decree for payment, other than expenses;
- (iv) an interlocutor making an order *ad factum praestandum;*
- (v)   an interlocutor sisting an action;
- (vi) an interlocutor allowing, refusing, or limiting the mode of proof;
- (vii) an interlocutor refusing a reponing note.

An appeal may be marked against any interlocutor which the sheriff, either *ex proprio motu* or on the motion of any party, grants leave to appeal (1907 Act, s 27).

2. Appeal to the Court of Session

The following interlocutors may be appealed from the Sheriff Principal or the sheriff to the Court of Session without leave:
    (i)   a final judgment (as defined above);
    (ii) an interlocutor granting an interim decree for payment of money other than a decree for expenses;
    (iii) an interlocutor sisting an action;
    (iv) an interlocutor refusing a reponing note.

An appeal may be marked against any interlocutor against which the Sheriff Principal or sheriff, either *ex proprio motu* or on the motion of any party, grants leave to appeal (1907 Act, s 28).

3. Time limit for appeal (r 91)

Any interlocutor which does not require leave to appeal against it, may be appealed within fourteen days of the date of the interlocutor, unless it has been extracted following a motion for early extract (see r 90 above).

4. Application for leave to appeal and appeal therefrom (r 92)

Interlocutors referred to at 1 and 2 above may be appealed without leave being granted. All other interlocutors may be appealed only with leave of the sheriff or Sheriff Principal as the case may be. Application for leave to appeal must be made within seven days of the date of the interlocutor against which it is desired to appeal. Application is not competent if the interlocutor has been extracted following a motion for early extract. If leave is granted, the appeal must be marked within seven days of the granting of leave.

5. Form of appeal and giving notice to parties (r 93)

The appeal takes the form of a written note on:
    (i)   the interlocutor sheet; or
    (ii) any other written record containing the interlocutor; or

(iii) a separate sheet lodged with the sheriff clerk.

It should be in the following terms:

"The [pursuer, applicant, claimant, defender, respondent or other
party] appeals to [the Sheriff Principal or The Court of Session]"
and should be signed by the appellant and show the date on which it is
signed.

If the appeal is to the Sheriff Principal, the sheriff should be requested to
append a note to his interlocutor, if he has not done so, by adding the
words "and requests the sheriff to write a note" (see r 89, page 85).

If the appeal is to the Court of Session the note of appeal must specify
the name and address of the solicitors in Edinburgh who will be acting
for the appellant.

Within four days of the appeal being marked the sheriff clerk must:
(i) send written notice of the appeal to all other parties to the
     cause and certify on the interlocutor sheet that he has done so;
     and
(ii) transmit the process to the Sheriff Principal or the Court of
     Session (Deputy Principal Clerk of Session) as the case may
     be.
Failure by the sheriff clerk to send notice or certify as above will not
invalidate the appeal.

6. Reclaiming petition or oral hearing (r 94)

An oral hearing is the most common procedure for an appeal before the
Sheriff Principal. He may order a reclaiming petition and answers in
which the arguments for parties are set out, but this method is almost
unknown in practice. If all parties are agreed that neither a reclaiming
petition nor an oral hearing is necessary, they may move the Sheriff
Principal to dispose of the appeal accordingly.

7. Interim possession pending appeal (r 95)

The judge against whose judgment an appeal is taken (Sheriff Principal

or sheriff), may make orders relating to:
  (i)   interim possession;
  (ii) the preservation of any property to which the action relates, or for its sale, if perishable;
  (iii) the preservation of evidence; or
  (iv) any matter which the judge considers necessary in the interests of parties.

These orders, once made, are not subject to reviews except by the Appellate Court (the Court of Session or Sheriff Principal).

8. Abandonment of appeal (r 96)

An appeal to the Sheriff Principal having been marked, it can be abandoned only with the consent of all parties or by leave of the Sheriff Principal. There is no procedure in the sheriff court for abandonment of an appeal marked to the Court of Session.

Chapter 15

Expenses

1. Decree for expenses extracted in solicitor's name (r 97)

If expenses are moved for in an undefended cause, it is normal practice to elect to charge an inclusive fee as fixed in the table of fees. This is an optional procedure - the pursuer may alternatively move for expenses as taxed by the auditor of court. This latter is the normal procedure in decrees *in foro*, in which case the sheriff allows an account of expenses to be given in and remits the account, when lodged, to the auditor of court to tax the account and report back to the court.

When the account of expenses has been taxed, the sheriff is asked to grant decree for the taxed amount. At this stage, the solicitor acting for the party moving for decree may ask the sheriff to allow the decree for expenses to be extracted in his name, the effect being that the solicitor can recover the expenses for himself separately from any other recovery action by the client against the debtor.

2. Taxation of expenses (r 98)

Where the sheriff has allowed an account of expenses to be remitted to the auditor of court for taxation:
  (i)   the account is lodged with the sheriff clerk;
  (ii) the account and process are transmitted by the sheriff clerk to the auditor of court;
  (iii) on receipt of the account, the auditor assigns a diet for the taxation not earlier than seven days from the date he receives the account;

(iv) the auditor intimates the diet forthwith to the party who lodged the account;

(v) the party who lodged the account must forthwith send a copy of the account to all other parties and advise them of the date, time and place fixed for the taxation;

(vi) any or all parties may decide not to attend the taxation;

(vii) if parties are present, they may make representation on the amount of any item in the account;

(viii) the auditor may conclude the taxation at the diet or adjourn the diet for further consideration, in which case, he must inform parties who attended the taxation of his decision;

(ix) when the account has been taxed, the auditor returns the process and account to the sheriff clerk;

(x) a note of objection to the taxed account may be lodged, but only by a party who attended the taxation; the note must be lodged within seven days of the taxation;

(xi) the sheriff must dispose of the objection in a summary manner, with or without answers being lodged by other parties; and

(xii) if no note of objection is lodged, the sheriff may grant decree for the expenses as taxed.

Chapter 16

Sequestration for rent

1. Introduction

The purpose of an ordinary action of sequestration for rent is to enable the landlord to recover rent arrears and future rent due. Moveable articles are sequestrated and sold and the proceeds paid to the landlord. If there are insufficient articles in the premises to meet the amount due, the tenant may be ordered to replenish the premises (ie to furnish the premises with effects of sufficient value to afford the pursuer security for future rent due), failing which he may face ejection.

2. Actions craving payment for rent (r 99)

The action may be raised before or after the term of payment, and the writ normally includes craves for sequestration:
    (i)   in security; or
    (ii) for payment of rent arrears; or
    (iii) for payment of rent to become due.

A crave for an order to replenish if insufficient moveables are found in the premises is normally included along with a crave for ejection failing replenishment. The action proceeds in the normal manner.

3. Warrant to inventory and secure (r 100)

If the sheriff is satisfied that a *prima facie* case has been made out, the first warrant includes an order sequestrating the effects of the tenant and granting warrant to inventory and secure them.

The procedure may include orders to sequestrate, to inventory and sell effects, to eject the tenant and to relet the premises. All of these orders include warrant to open shut and lockfast places.

4. Sale of effects (r 101)

The warrant of sale:
  (i) will not be granted until the term for payment of rent has passed;
  (ii) authorises sale of so many of the effects as will meet the rent, interest and expenses;
  (iii) specifies where and when the sale will take place and the method of advertising the sale;
  (iv) directs the sale to proceed at the sight of an officer of court or other named person, eg an auctioneer.

The report of sale:
  (i) is lodged with the sheriff clerk by the pursuer within fourteen days of the sale;
  (ii) includes the roup rolls, or certified copies, and a state of debt.

If there are surplus proceeds, these are lodged with the sheriff clerk and repaid to the tenant.

If there is a deficit, the pursuer may apply for a decree for the amount of deficit or for an order for the tenant to replenish the premises. If the tenant fails to replenish, the pursuer may apply for warrant to eject the tenant and to relet the premises.

5. Care of effects (r 102)

At any stage of the proceedings the sheriff may:
  (i) appoint a fit person to take charge of the sequestrated effects; or
  (ii) require the tenant to find caution (security) that they shall be made available.

Chapter 17

Removing

1. Introduction

An ordinary action of removing is the process by which a tenant, whose right to occupancy has come to an end, is judicially warned to remove from the premises occupied by him, failing which he is liable to be ejected.

In this chapter, the term "ejection" is used to describe the diligence following a decree of removing or the actual carrying out of the removing. This is distinct from an ordinary action of ejection, which is the process by which a person occupying heritable subjects without any right or title such as a squatter, is ejected therefrom. The 1907 Act also contains authority for ejection without recourse to the court (ss 34 and 35) and for warrant to eject without first obtaining a decree of removal (ss 36 and 37). These are classed as removings and are dealt with in this chapter.

A notice of removal (by the landlord) or letter of removal (by the tenant) is a prerequisite to an action of removing.

2. Ordinary action of removing (r 103)

An ordinary action may be raised at any time provided:
    (i)   the tenant has bound himself to remove by writing, dated and signed within twelve months of the term of removal; or
    (ii) where he has not so bound himself:
        •   in the case of a lease for three years and upwards, of lands exceeding two acres, not less than one year and not more than two years elapse between notice of removal and term

of removal;

- in the case of the lease of such lands, written or verbal, from year to year under tacit relocation or for less than three years, an interval of not less than six months elapses between notice of removal and term of removal; or

(iii) in the case of:

- houses with or without land not exceeding two acres;
- land not exceeding two acres without houses;
- mills, fishings and shootings; and
- all other heritable subjects excepting land exceeding two acres and let for one year or more;

forty days elapse between notice of removal and term of removal.

These provisions do not apply to subjects falling under the Agricultural Holdings (Scotland) Act 1949 of which s 24 has provision as to giving notice to quit.

In any defended ordinary action of removing, the sheriff may order the defender to find caution for violent profits, for example to cover damage done by the defender or the profit which the landlord could have made out of the subjects. If caution is ordered but not found, decree of removal may be pronounced forthwith.

In an action of irritancy and removing by a superior against a vassal, the pursuer must call as parties the last entered vassal and such heritable creditors and holders of postponed ground burdens as are disclosed by a search for twenty years prior to the action. The cost of the search forms part of the pursuer's expenses of process.

The forms of notices, service of notices and evidence of notices under this rule are not prescribed, but rr 104-107 should be applied, subject to modification as necessary.

3. Removing without recourse to the court

(a) Probative lease (s 34 of the 1907 Act)

This procedure applies to land:

(i)   which exceeds two acres; and

(ii)   is held under a probative (presumed genuine without further proof) lease specifying a term of endurance.

Notice to remove must be in writing (in terms of Form L in the schedule to the rules) and must be given:

(i)   where the lease is for three years and upwards, not less than one year and not more than two years before the termination of the lease; and

(ii)   in the case of leases from year to year, including lands occupied by tacit relocation, or for any period less than three years, not less than six months before the termination of the lease (or where there is a separate ish as regards land and houses or otherwise, before that ish which is first in date).

For the procedure for service and certification of notices to remove, see rr 106 and 107, page 99.

If the above conditions are satisfied, the lease, or an extract if it has been recorded in the books of court, has the same force and effect as a decree of removing obtained in an ordinary action. Written authority by the landlord, or anyone authorised by him, is sufficient warrant for a sheriff officer or messenger-at-arms to eject the tenant and there being no decree, there is no need to serve a charge. The removal or ejection must be executed not later than six weeks from the date of the latest ish.

(b)   *Letter of removal (s 35 of the 1907 Act)*

This procedure applies to lands which:

(i)   exceed two acres;

(ii)   are in the possession of a tenant, with or without a written lease; and where the tenant has signed a letter of removal (in terms of Form M in the schedule to the rules) at the date of entering or at any other time which is holograph or attested by one witness.

In these circumstances, the letter has the same force and effect as a decree of removing in an ordinary action. For the procedure for service and certification of the letter of removal, see rr 106 and 107 below.

If the above conditions are satisfied, the letter is sufficient warrant for ejection and can be implemented in the same manner and within the same time limit as in *(a)* above (probative lease).

4. Summary warrant

(a) Land exceeding two acres (s 36 of the 1907 Act)

This procedure applies in the case of lands exceeding two acres where:
>   (i)   there is no written lease; and
>   (ii) no letter of removal has been granted by the tenant.

The tenancy may be ended by written notice, given by either side, not less than six months before the termination of the tenancy. The notice should be in terms of Form L in the schedule to the rules (see page 145), suitably amended if given by the tenant. If the tenant fails to remove, the landlord may apply to the court for a summary warrant of ejection. This is an ordinary action and the normal rules of procedure apply.

(b) Lands let for a year or more (s 37 of the 1907 Act)

In cases of:
>   (i)   houses, with or without land attached not exceeding two acres;
>   (ii)   lands not exceeding two acres let without houses;
>   (iii) mills, fishings and shootings;
>   (iv)   all other heritable subjects excepting land exceeding two acres,

let for a year or more, notice of termination of the tenancy may be given by one or other of the parties. Notice (in terms of Form N in the schedule to the rules (see pages 145-146), suitably adapted when used by the tenant), must be given at least forty days before:
>   (i)   the fifteenth day of May when the termination of the tenancy is the term of Whit-Sunday; or
>   (ii) the eleventh day of November when the termination is the term of Martinmas.

If the tenant fails to remove, the landlord may apply to the court for a warrant of summary ejection. This is an ordinary action and the normal rules of procedure apply.

5. Removal notices (r 106)

Removal notices under ss 34, 35, 36 or 37 of the 1907 Act may be given by:
  (i)   a sheriff officer or messenger-at-arms; or
  (ii) registered letter or recorded delivery post by the person entitled to give notice, or the solicitor or factor of such person.

The notice, if posted, must be posted in time to admit of its being delivered at or prior to the last date on which notice must be given. It should be addressed to the person entitled to receive it and should bear his particular address at the time, if known, or, if not known, his last known address.

6. Evidence of notice to remove (r 107)

(a) Lease or letter of removal

The following constitute sufficient evidence that notice has been given:
  (i)   a certificate that notice has been given in cases under s 34, 35 or 36 endorsed on:
    •   the lease or extract; or
    •   the letter of removal
    by the sheriff officer, messenger-at-arms, person giving notice or the solicitor or factor of such person; or
  (ii) an acknowledgment of notice endorsed as above, by the party in possession or his agent.

(b) No lease or letter of removal

A certificate endorsed on a copy notice or letter (certified correct) by the person, sheriff officer, messenger-at-arms, solicitor or factor sending the notice or letter and signed by such party is sufficient evidence that notice has been given.

(c) Notice or letter under s 37 of the 1907 Act

A certificate of notice to remove or letter of removal, dated and endorsed on a copy of the notice or letter, signed by the party sending the notice is sufficient evidence that notice has been given.

7. Charge

No charge (see page 37) is necessary before the execution of diligence in applications under ss 34 or 35 of the 1907 Act, there being no decree or order of court.

Cases proceeding under ss 36 or 37 of the 1907 Act and r 103 are ordinary actions and if decree is granted, a charge is necessary. However, there is doubt on the number of days of charge. The rules provide (r 13) that any charge following, or a decree granted in, an ordinary cause shall be for a period of fourteen days.

Extracts of decrees of removing are regulated by s 7(4) of the Sheriff Courts (Scotland) Extracts Act 1892 and Form 10 in the schedule to that Act, and the period of charge is 48 hours.

Practice may vary from court to court.

Chapter 18

Summary suspension

1. General

The sheriff court has jurisdiction to suspend charges or threatened charges on decrees granted by the sheriff or on decrees of registration proceeding on bonds, bills, contracts or other obligations registered in the books of the sheriff court, the books of council and session or any other competent registers. Suspension of the charge prevents implementation of the decree until an alleged illegality is inquired into or the rights of parties finally determined. Summary suspension proceeds by way of a summary application, as defined in s 3(p) of the 1907 Act. The application is disposed of in a summary manner - a diet is fixed and intimated to the defender, answers are ordered and, if necessary, a hearing is fixed and judgment issued. The procedure is restricted to a charge on decrees as defined below (see r 108).

For "charge" see page 37. "Letters of horning" are issued by the sheriff clerk following registration of a decree in the register of hornings. The effect of registration is to accumulate debt and interest into one capital sum on which interest runs from the date of registration.

2. Summary application for suspension of a charge (r 108)

Where a charge has been executed on:
  (i)   a decree granted by the sheriff;
  (ii) a decree of registration of a bond, bill or other form of obligation, registered in the books of a sheriff court, the books of council and session or any others competent; or

(iii) letters of horning following on a decree as above,
for payment of a sum of money, the person charged may apply to the
sheriff having jurisdiction over him for suspension of the charge and
diligence.

3. Sist of diligence (r 109)

The sheriff fixes the amount of caution to cover any expenses incurred
in the suspension process and orders such caution, plus caution for the
amount of the sum charged for with interest and expenses, to be found
in the hands of the sheriff clerk, in a specified time. Caution having
been found, the sheriff may suspend the charge and sist further diligence.
If he does so, a diet is fixed, the initial writ is intimated to the defender
(served on him) and he is appointed to lodge answers, if so advised. The
case is disposed of in a summary manner.

4. Objections (r 110)

Any decision of the sheriff on objections to the competency or
regularity of the suspension proceedings may be appealed to the Sheriff
Principal whose decision is final. An appeal on the merits is not
excluded by this rule (for the procedure, see Chapter 14).

Chapter 19

Arrestment

1. General

Arrestment is the procedure by which a creditor attaches moveable property belonging to the debtor but which is in the hands of a third party. It is executed by a sheriff officer serving a schedule of arrestment on the third party (the arrestee). The schedule may be served personally or by post.

2. Service of schedule of arrestment (r 111)

If a schedule of arrestment has not been served personally on an arrestee then:

   (i)   in the case of an individual arrestee a copy of the schedule of arrestment must be sent by post (registered or recorded delivery) to:
   - the last known place of residence of the arrestee; or
   - if this is unknown, to the arrestee's principal place of business if known; or
   - if this is unknown, to any known place of business; and

   (ii) in the case of a firm or corporation, the schedule must be sent by post (as above) to:
   - the principal place of business, if known; or
   - if this is unknown, to any known place of business.

In his execution of service of the arrestment, the officer of court must describe the method and specify the address to which the copy has been sent.

3. Report of arrestment (r 112)

If an arrestment on the dependence of an action is used prior to service, the action must be served within twenty days of the arrestment and:
  (i)   in defended cases the cause must be tabled within twenty days of the first ordinary court day occurring after the expiry of the period of notice; or
  (ii) in undefended cases, decree in absence must be taken within twenty days of the expiry of the period of notice,
otherwise the arrestment falls.

Where an arrestment on the dependence has been executed, the party using it or his agent (the officer of court) must forthwith report the execution to the sheriff clerk.

Chapter 20

Multiplepoinding

1. Introduction

The purpose of an action of multiplepoinding is to determine the rights in a fund or subject, known as the fund *in medio*, on which there are two or more competing claims.

The fund *in medio* may consist of moveables, moveable rights, heritage or heritable rights. It often consists of money.

The action may be raised by the holder of the fund, who asks the court to decide how the fund should be distributed or by a claimant on the fund whose claim has been refused by the holder.

2. Initial writ (rr 113 116)

The holder of the fund should be identified in the instance of the initial writ as follows:
- (i) if the holder of the fund raises the action, the instance should read:

  AB (*design*) holder of the fund *in medio*, Pursuer; or
- (ii) if a claimant on the fund raises the action, the instance should read:

  CD (*design*) claimant on the fund *in medio*, Pursuer against
  EF (*design*) holder of the fund *in medio*, Defender.

All known claimants on the fund or other interested parties should be called as defenders.

If the pursuer is the holder of the fund, the condescendence of the initial writ should contain a detailed description of the fund *in medio*.

3. Service (rr 114, 115 and 125)

The warrant to cite does not follow the usual style. If the defenders intend to lodge:
  (i) defences to the competency of the action;
  (ii) objections to the condescendence of the fund *in medio* (if this has been included in the initial writ); or
  (iii) a claim on the fund *in medio*,
they are directed to lodge a notice of appearance (not a notice of intention to defend) (see below).

Service is ordered on all parties known to have an interest in the fund (this will generally mean the defenders), including the holder of the fund where the pursuer is not the holder.

It is possible that there will be unknown claimants on the fund and, to cover this, the sheriff may include in the warrant to cite a direction that the import of the initial writ should be advertised in such newspapers as he considers necessary.

4. Notice of appearance (r 117)

Any party intending to lodge one or more of the documents mentioned in 3 above, must lodge a notice of appearance in terms of Form O in the schedule to the rules, before the expiry of the period of notice.

5. Tabling (rr 118, 119 and 120)

If appearance is entered, the pursuer must make up a process and lodge it for tabling in the usual way (see page 52).

If the holder of the fund is not the pursuer, the sheriff, on tabling, appoints a period within which the holder is to lodge a detailed condescendence of the fund *in medio*, together with a list of all persons, so far as known to him, who have an interest in the fund.

At tabling, an assessment is made of the various interests of the parties who have entered appearance. The sheriff appoints a period within which defences, objections or claims must be lodged.

The case is continued to a later date on the procedure roll.

Defences, objections or claims may be combined in one document under separate headings, and claims should be accompanied by any document founded on, if within the custody or power of the claimant.

6. Defences (r 121)

If defences have been lodged, they must be disposed of before the action can proceed. The sheriff fixes a period for the adjustment of the initial writ and the defences, after which the record is closed and the action proceeds as an ordinary cause (see r 62, page 65). Thereafter, assuming that the case has not been otherwise disposed of, it will be re-enrolled on the procedure roll.

If no defences have been lodged, or having been lodged they have been disposed of, the next stage in the procedure concerns objections to the fund *in medio*.

7. Objections (r 122)

If objections have been lodged, the sheriff fixes a period for the adjustment of the condescendence of the fund and objections after which the record is closed and the action proceeds as an ordinary cause (see r 62, page 65).

If no objections have been lodged, or having been lodged they have been disposed of, the sheriff, without order for intimation to any other party, may, on the motion of the holder of the fund, approve the condescendence of the fund and find the holder liable only in once and single payment.

8. Claims

Claims on the fund *in medio* must be in writing and should comprise a condescendence of facts, a formal claim to a stated share of the fund and pleas-in-law.

9. Consignation (rr 123 and 124)

The sheriff, having approved the condescendence of the fund *in medio*, may order it to be consigned or deposited with the sheriff clerk. If the fund or part of it is not easily divisible, the sheriff may order the whole or part of the fund to be sold and the proceeds consigned with the sheriff clerk.

When the holder has consigned or deposited the fund, he may apply for his exoneration and discharge and when this has been granted, the sheriff may allow the holder his expenses out of the fund as a first charge on it.

10. Further service (r 125)

At this stage the fund has been consigned, but before ordering division and payment, the sheriff may order further advertisement or service on any person if it is doubtful if all possible claimants are aware of the action.

11. Ranking of claims (r 126)

When the holder of the fund has been exonorated and discharged and has consigned the fund he is no longer involved in the process. The next stage is to decide how the fund should be divided among the claimants.

Claims may be lodged at a late stage in the proceedings (see r 125 above). If all claimants are agreed on the division of the fund the sheriff will rank and prefer claimants in terms of their claims. However, if there is competition among claimants, the sheriff fixes a period for the adjustment of claims after which the record is closed and the action proceeds as an ordinary cause (see r 62, page 65).

12. Remit to reporter (r 127)

If he considers it to be necessary, the sheriff may remit the case to a reporter to prepare a scheme of division and report back. The expenses of the remit, when approved by the sheriff, are a charge on the fund to be deducted before division.

13. Final procedure

Before making payment to claimants, the sheriff clerk may require the exhibition of tax clearance certificates in terms of the Act of Sederunt of 16 July 1936.

Chapter 21

Miscellaneous matters

1. Disposal of money payable to persons under legal disability (r 128)

This rule operates where a court has granted decree in an action of damages for personal injury or death and a sum of money is payable to a person under legal disability, in which case the money is paid into court and administered by the sheriff clerk.

A typical example is where a father has been fatally injured in the course of his employment and his minor or pupil children have been awarded damages.

If the legal disability is removed, for example by the person attaining majority, all sums accrued are paid to the entitled person.

Where in an action of damages by or on behalf of a person under legal disability arising out of:
  (i)   injury sustained by such person; or
  (ii) the death of some other person in respect of whose death the person under legal disability is entitled to damages,
a sum of money is payable to such person, the sum, unless otherwise directed, is paid into court and invested and administered by the court for the benefit of such person.

The receipt of the sheriff clerk is sufficient discharge in respect of the amount paid in.

The sheriff clerk is authorised to accept custody of money paid into any competent court in any (unrestricted) action of damages by or on behalf of a person under legal disability, provided that such person resides within the jurisdiction of the sheriff court; the money is then administered as above.

The money is paid out or applied for the benefit of the entitled person as the sheriff may direct. Payments may be regular for fixed amounts, occasional for specific purposes, or no request for payments may be made.

When the money is paid into court, the sheriff clerk issues a receipt in terms of Form P in the schedule to the rules, and Form Q is attached to the receipt. A copy of Form P accompanied by Form R is sent to Scottish Courts Administration by the sheriff clerk and Form Q is sent to Scottish Courts Administration by the person making payment. The purpose of this procedure is to make the transaction secure.

Investment of the money is restricted to the way in which trustees are authorised to invest by virtue of the Trustee Investment Act 1961.

2. Recall or variation of decrees and orders (r 129)

Variation or recall of decrees for payment of aliment, orders for financial provision and decrees regulating the custody of or access to children depends on whether or not there is an action pending before a court. If no action is pending, application for:

(i)   the recall or variation of a sheriff court decree for payment of aliment;

(ii) recall or variation of a periodical allowance;

(iii) variation of the date or method of payment of a capital sum;

(iv) variation of the date of transfer of property;

(v)   recall or variation of a decree for custody of or access to children; or

(vi) recall or variation of an incidental order as defined in s 14(2) of the Family Law (Scotland) Act 1985 whenever made

may be made by minute in the original process in which the decree was granted or the order made.

The minute is served on the opposite party or parties who are given a specific time within which to lodge answers, if so advised. The record is not closed. The sheriff decides on the appropriate procedure, including proof if necessary, and disposes of the application.

In a pending action of divorce or of separation, either party may crave an order relating to custody of, access to, or aliment for, children of the marriage, or aliment for one of the parties notwithstanding that such an order has been made in the same or another sheriff court. A new order supersedes the previous order.

A change of circumstances is normally a prerequisite to applications for variation or recall of decrees and orders.

The sheriff has power to vary or recall certain orders made by the Court of Session in respect of maintenance, custody and the like - see s 8 of the Law Reform (Miscellanous Provisions) (Scotland) Act 1966.

3. Intimations to third parties (r 130)

This rule provides for intimation being sent to parties who may have an interest in the action but who were not parties in the action when it was first raised. It also specifies the procedure under which a third party, having received intimation, may apply for leave to enter the action. Cases in which intimation is required and the procedure are described below.

The need for intimation is identified by the sheriff clerk when the initial writ is first lodged. The order for intimation may be included in the warrant to cite, or it may be made at a later stage in the proceedings, and a separate provision on citation applies in cases where the pursuer alleges sodomy or any homosexual relationship between the defender and a named person. Intimation is made in terms of the various Forms in the schedule to the rules and, in most cases, a copy of the initial writ is served on the third party.

The standard period of notice is fourteen days unless varied by the sheriff but in no case is it less than 48 hours.

If so advised, the third party may apply by minute to be sisted as a party to the action and for leave to lodge defences or answers. A diet for hearing the application is fixed by the sheriff clerk for a date after the expiry of the period of notice. The sheriff may grant or refuse the application and may regulate the procedure as he thinks fit, including authorising proof by affidavit evidence in any matter not in dispute.

The rules provide for intimation in the following circumstances:

(a)   Adultery (intimation in terms of Form H1)

Where the initial writ or the defences contain an allegation that either party has committed adultery with a named person who is not a party to the action, a copy of the initial writ and a form of intimation must be sent to such person, unless the sheriff is satisfied that such person's address is unknown.

(b)   Sodomy or homosexual relationship (Form H2)

Where the pursuer alleges sodomy or a homosexual relationship between the defender and a named person who is not a party to the action, no intimation is ordered until the period of notice has expired, when the pursuer must enrol a motion for an order for intimation. The sheriff may order intimation or dispense with it. In the latter case, he may also order that the name of the third party be deleted from the condescendence in the initial writ. If intimation is ordered, a form of intimation and a copy of the initial writ is sent to the third party.

(c)   Polygamy (Form H4)

In actions for divorce or separation relating to a marriage entered into under a law which permits polygamy, and either party has a spouse who is not a party to the cause, intimation is ordered on every additional spouse whose address is known, and a form of intimation and a copy of the initial writ is sent.

(d)   Transfer of property under s 8(1) of the Family Law (Scotland) Act 1985 (Form H7)

In actions for divorce in which an order is sought by the pursuer or the defender for transfer of property which is subject to security and the consent of the creditor has not been obtained, the party seeking the order must send a form of intimation and a copy of the initial writ to the creditor.

(e) Custody of and maintenance of children

Intimation to third parties in actions relating to custody of or maintenance of children must be made in the following circumstances:

(i) where the child is in the care of a local authority (Form H3);

(ii) where the child is liable to be maintained by the third party (Form H3);

(iii) where the child is in *de facto* custody of the third party (Form H5); and

(iv) where the sheriff proposes to commit the care of the child to a third party or a local authority (Form H6).

In the above cases the form of intimation must be accompanied by a copy of the initial writ and are both sent by the pursuer.

If the sheriff makes an order placing the child under the supervision of a local authority, the sheriff clerk sends intimation to the local authority in terms of Form H6A with a certified copy of the interlocutor.

In an action for custody of a child by any relative, step-parent or foster parent of the child, by virtue of s 47 of the Children Act 1975, that person must give notice:

(i) to the local authority within whose area that person resides within seven days of lodging the action; or

(ii) to such local authority and within such time as the court may specify.

Notice is given by sending a copy of the initial writ and intimation in terms of Form T2.

(f) Minutes

A third party who has received intimation and who wishes to be sisted as a party to the action must lodge a minute with the sheriff clerk for leave to join the action as a party and to lodge defences or answers. The minute, accompanied by the service copy of the intimation, must be lodged within fourteen days from the date of posting of the intimation. When the minute is lodged, the sheriff clerk enrols the cause for a hearing, on a date after the expiry of the period of notice, and the sheriff, at the hearing, regulates further procedure.

4. Notices in actions of divorce and separation (r 131)

Ordinary actions of divorce or of separation may be raised:

(i) after non-cohabitation between the pursuer and defender for a continuous period of two years where the defender consents to decree; or

(ii) without consent of the defender where the continuous period of non-cohabitation is for a period of five years or more.

The circumstances on which the action is based are narrated in the condescendence in the normal way.

Service of the initial writ includes statutory notices which are designed to inform the defender of such matters as the effect of decree and consent (where appropriate) including withdrawal of consent.

Notice or notices (in terms of Forms in the schedule) to be sent with the service copy initial writ depend on the type of action.

Separation

(i) two years' non-cohabitation and consent: Forms S & T

(ii) five years' non-cohabitation: Form S2

Divorce

(i) two years' non-cohabitation and consent: Forms S1 and T

(ii) five years' non-cohabitation - Form S3

5. Consent to grant of decree (r 132)

In actions of divorce or of separation where the defender's consent to decree is necessary (see r 131 above) a form of consent is enclosed with the service copy initial writ. If the defender consents to decree he or she is required to sign Form T. The completed form is sent to the sheriff clerk who lodges it in process.

If the defender does not consent to decree, or if he or she wishes to withdraw a consent already given, the defender should give notice in writing to the sheriff clerk, who intimates the terms of the notice to the pursuer.

The next stage in the procedure depends on whether or not the initial writ contains other averments that there has been an irretrievable breakdown in the marriage, for example that the defender has committed adultery; and if so the action will proceed in the normal way. If there are no such averments, the pursuer must enrol a motion to have the action sisted and the sheriff may grant the motion. If procedure has been sisted and the sist has been neither recalled nor renewed within a period of six months from the grant of the sist, the pursuer is deemed to have abandoned the action.

6. Application under the Family Law (Scotland) Act 1985 (r 132A)

Some applications under this rule may be made as part of a pending action while others are made by separate summary application.

Where, in any pending action in which an alimentary crave exists or may be made, any party seeks to vary or terminate a related agreement on aliment, application may be made in the initial writ or by a separate minute in process. Where there is no such action pending, application may be made by summary application.

Where a party seeks an order setting aside or varying any term of an agreement relating to a periodical allowance, application may be made by summary application.

Where a party in a pending action of divorce seeks an order that an agreement or financial provision was not fair or reasonable at the time it was entered into, application may be made in the initial writ or by minute in process or, where appropriate, by way of counterclaim.

7. Applications to declare removal of a child unlawful (r 132B)

Where, in custody proceedings, the sheriff has made a decision relating to the care of the person of a child, to the right to decide on the place of the child's residence or the right of access to the child and that child has been removed from the United Kingdom, any interested person may apply to the sheriff for declarator that the removal of the child was unlawful. The application may be made in the initial writ or counterclaim, or by separate minute in the process.

8. Appointment of curator ad litem (r 133)

The purpose of this rule is to afford protection to a defender, in an action of divorce or of separation, who may be suffering from mental disorder within the meaning of the Mental Health (Scotland) Act 1984 and also to overcome the possible difficulty of obtaining written consent from the defender in such circumstances.

Where it appears to the sheriff that the defender is suffering from mental disorder, as mentioned above, the sheriff must appoint a curator *ad litem* (a person appointed by the court to look after the defender's interests in the action), and the pursuer must send a certified copy of the initial writ and defences (if any) to the curator within seven days of the appointment.

If the action is for divorce on the basis of two years' non-cohabitation and the consent of the defender is required, the sheriff will make an order informing the Mental Welfare Commission for Scotland and requesting it to report on whether the defender is capable of deciding whether or not to give consent to the granting of decree.

Within fourteen days of the Commission submitting a report or, if no report has been called for, within 21 days of his appointment, the curator may lodge:
- (i) a notice of appearance;
- (ii) defences;
- (iii) a minute adopting defences already lodged; or
- (iv) a minute stating that he does not intend to lodge defences.

In any event, the curator may appear in the action at any time to protect the interests of the defender.

Notice of the action must be sent to the curator *bonis* (a person appointed by the court to manage the affairs of a person who is incapable of doing so, eg by reason of mental illness), if any, and where the defender is resident in a hospital or similar institution, to the medical officer in charge - see r 11A, page 33.

9. The European Court (r 134)

Rule 134 applies to references to the Court of Justice of the European Communities for preliminary rulings:
   (i)   under art 177 of the European Economic Community Treaty;
   (ii) under art 150 of the European Atomic Energy Community Treaty;
   (iii) under art 41 of the European Coal and Steel Community Treaty; or
   (iv) on the conventions as defined in s 1(1) of the Civil Jurisdiction and Judgments Act 1982, under art 3 of Sch 2 to that Act.

A reference may be made by the sheriff *ex proprio motu*, or on the motion of any party to the proceedings, for a preliminary ruling on the interpretation of the treaties or the interpretation, validity etc of acts, statutes or institutions established under the treaties, where such interpretation, validity etc is in issue in the proceedings before the sheriff.

When the sheriff has decided that a reference should be made, the case is continued *simpliciter* and the sheriff drafts a reference, in terms of Form U in the schedule, within four weeks.

The sheriff clerk sends a copy of the draft reference to each party.

Within four weeks of the issue of the draft reference, each party may lodge adjustments with the sheriff clerk and, at the same time, send a copy to each of the other parties.

Within fourteen days after the latest date on which adjustments either are or could be lodged the sheriff, after considering any adjustments, must make and sign the reference and this step is intimated to the parties by the sheriff clerk.

Provided that no appeal procedure is involved (see below), a copy of the reference, certified by the sheriff clerk, is transmitted by the sheriff clerk to the Registrar of the European Court.

Unless the sheriff otherwise orders, procedure in the action is sisted until the European Court has given a preliminary ruling, but the sheriff may recall the sist to make any interim order which a due regard to the interests of the parties may require.

Unless the sheriff otherwise directs, a reference shall not be sent to the European Court if:
- (i)   the time for applying for leave to appeal or for marking an appeal has not expired; or
- (ii) an appeal having been marked has not been disposed of.

Chapter 22

Simplified divorce procedure

1. Introduction

This is a cheap and simple method of obtaining a decree of divorce in certain uncontested actions (see r 135 below). As in all divorce actions, it must be established that there has been an irretrievable breakdown in the marriage, but for the simplified procedure to operate, the reason for the divorce is restricted to the non-cohabitation of the parties over certain periods of time. The written consent of the defender may or may not be necessary, depending on the length of the period of non-cohabitation.

The popular name for the procedure is "do-it-yourself" because the forms, which are obtainable from the sheriff clerk, are designed for completion by the applicant personally, although they may also be lodged by solicitors.

The grounds of jurisdiction are tiered at national and local levels. An action of divorce is competent under simplified procedure if:

    (i)   either party to the marriage is domiciled in Scotland at the date when the action is begun; or

    (ii)   either party was habitually resident in Scotland throughout the period of one year ending with the date when the action is begun;

AND

    (iii) either party was resident in the sheriffdom for a period of forty days ending on the date when the action is begun; or

    (iv) •   the pursuer (applicant) resides furth of Scotland and has been resident in the sheriffdom for a period of not less than forty days ending not more than forty days before the date when the action is begun; or

- the defender (respondent) has been resident in the sheriffdom for at least forty days ending not more than forty days before the action is begun and has no known residence in Scotland at that date.

2. Simplified procedure (r 135)

Applications under simplified procedure must satisfy the following conditions:

(i) • two years' non-cohabitation and the defender consents to decree; or
- five years' non-cohabitation
(see below for calculation of periods of non-cohabitation);
(ii) no other proceedings are pending in any court which could have the effect of bringing the marriage to an end;
(iii) there are no children of the marriage under 16 years of age;
(iv) neither party applies for an order for financial provision; and
(v) neither party suffers from mental disorder within the meaning of the Mental Health (Scotland) Act 1984.

If an application to the court fails to satisfy all of the above conditions at any time before it is finally disposed of, it must be dismissed.

In calculating the periods of non-cohabitation, no account is taken of any period or periods, not exceeding six months in all, during which the parties co-habit (in an attempt at reconciliation). For example, if during the period of non-cohabitation, there has been co-habitation for a period of five months, application may be made not earlier than two years and five months or five years and five months, as the case may be, from the date of the original separation.

3. Forms of application (r 136)

Forms of application, which are specified in the schedule to the rules, are available on request from the sheriff clerk. The forms (with sheriff court numbers in brackets) are:

- SDA1 (SP2): application based on two years' non-cohabitation; and
- SDA2 (SP5): application based on five years' non-cohabit-

ation.

A guide to simplified procedure (SP1) is issued with each form.

The applicant must complete the following procedure before lodging the application with the sheriff clerk:

(a) *Two years non-cohabitation*

Part 1 of the form must be completed and signed by the applicant, after which the form, together with Form SP3 (issued with SP2) is sent to the respondent by the applicant for completion and signature of part 2 of the form - the consent to divorce. Thereafter the form is returned to the applicant. If the respondent does not complete and sign the consent, the application cannot proceed. If the respondent has completed and signed the consent, the applicant must complete the affidavit in part 3 of the form. This is sworn before a justice of the peace, a notary public or a commissioner for oaths after which the application is lodged with the sheriff clerk (see r 137 below).

(b) *Five years non-cohabitation*

The procedure in this case is identical to that described above except that there is no need to obtain a signed consent from the respondent. When parts 1 and 2 have been completed, the application is lodged with the sheriff clerk.

A problem will arise if the respondent's address is unknown. In a two year non-cohabitation case the application cannot proceed without the signed consent of the respondent. In five year cases a remedy is provided in the rules (see r 138, page 124).

4. Lodging applications (r 137)

Completed applications should be lodged (by post or by hand) with the sheriff clerk together with:
    (i)   an extract or certified copy of the marriage certificate; and
    (ii) the correct fee.

This rule differs from r 3 (see page 26) which requires an extract of the relevant entry in the register of marriages to be lodged in an action of divorce or separation commenced by initial writ. A certified copy of the marriage certificate (rare, if not unknown, in practice) would be accepted in an application lodged under simplified procedure.

The sheriff clerk will advise on the amount of the fee. In certain circumstances, applicants may be exempted from payment of a fee. An explanatory leaflet (SP1A) is issued with the guide (SP1) and the exemption claim form (SP15).

5. Citation (r 138)

In simplified procedure citations or intimations are issued, in the first instance, by the sheriff clerk. Procedure varies depending on whether or not the address of the respondent is known.

(a) Address of respondent known

In both two year and five year cases a photocopy of the application is sent to the respondent together with a citation advising him that the application has been lodged, that he may oppose it by putting reasons in writing and sending a letter to the sheriff clerk and that he may exercise a right to claim a financial award.

The documents are sent by post and the envelope has the normal instructions regarding non-delivery printed on it (see page 38).

Service proceeds on a period of notice which commences on the day of posting. Where the period of notice expires on a Saturday, Sunday or public holiday, it is deemed to expire the first following day on which the sheriff clerk's office is open for civil court business.

The periods of notice are:
  (i)   14 days when the addressee is resident or has a place of business in the United Kingdom, the Isle of Man, the Channel Islands or the Republic of Ireland;
  (ii) 28 days when the addressee is resident or has a place of business outwith the above locations but is resident or has a place of business elsewhere in Europe; and
  (iii) 42 days when the addressee is resident or has a place of

business outside Europe.

The sheriff may shorten or extend the period of notice but at least two days notice must be given.

If postal service fails, the sheriff clerk obtains an estimate of the fee for service by sheriff officer. The applicant is advised that, if the action is to proceed, service by officer is necessary and that the fee for service must be paid in advance by the applicant.

Service by officer may be personal or by leaving in the hands of an inmate or employee at the dwelling place or place of business - but see also r 139, below.

(b) Address of respondent unknown

This situation may arise in five year cases. If so, the applicant is directed, in the form, to:
  (i)   state the name, address and relationship of one of the next-of-kin of the respondent;
  (ii) state the names, dates of birth and addresses of all children of the marriage, and whether the marriage took place in Scotland;
  (iii) obtain a letter from the General Register Office (Scotland) to the effect that there is no record of the respondent having divorced the applicant.

A photocopy of the application and a notice in terms of Form SDA7 in the schedule to the rules are sent by post to the next-of-kin and children of the marriage whose addresses are known. If the addresses of the next-of-kin or children are unknown, a notice in terms of Form SDA6 is posted on the Walls of Court.

6. Citation of or service on persons outwith Scotland (r 139)

The method of service on persons outwith Scotland depends on the residence or place of business or location of the persons. It also depends on whether or not a Convention on the service of documents exists between the United Kingdom and the country concerned. Sheriff clerks will advise on the existence of a convention. Apart from the fact that the sheriff clerk effects service under this rule, the method of citation and service is similar to that dealt with in Chapter 4.

7. Opposition to applications (r 140)

Any person who has been cited or to whom intimation has been made may:
   (i)   challenge the jurisdiction of the court; or
   (ii) oppose the grant of decree
by letter, lodged within the period of notice, giving reasons for opposition. If there is opposition and the sheriff decides that it is not frivolous, the application must be dismissed. All decisions on opposition are intimated by the sheriff clerk to all parties concerned with the application. The lodging of a letter as described does not imply acceptance of the jurisdiction of the court.

8. Decree (r 141)

If the application is in order, the sheriff grants decree on the expiry of the period of notice. The sheriff clerk posts an extract of the decree to each party not sooner than fourteen days after the grant of decree.

If the application has been served in a country to which the 1965 Hague Convention applies (see page 44), the sheriff must also be satisfied that service has been effected:
   (i)   in terms of r 139; or
   (ii) in a way which conforms to the following conditions:
- the document was transmitted by one of the methods provided for in the Convention;
- a period of not less than six months (as may be considered adequate by the sheriff) has elapsed since the date of transmission of the document; and
- no certificate of any kind has been received even though every reasonable effort has been made to obtain it through the competent authorities of the state addressed.

9. Appeal (r 142)

A respondent may appeal against the interlocutor granting decree within fourteen days of the grant by addressing a letter to the court giving reasons for the appeal.

10. Subsequent applications (r 143)

After the grant of decree, a party to the application may, on a change of circumstances of one or other or both parties, make a subsequent application to the sheriff in respect of any matter by lodging a minute in the original process.

Chapter 23

Damages

1. Action for damages under the Damages (Scotland) Act 1976 (r 144)

This rule and rr 145 and 146 apply to actions for damages arising from the death of a person from personal injuries. Where there is a possibility of separate actions being raised by claimants against the same defender, these rules provide that, in the event of an action being raised, notice is given to all possible claimants so that, in the interest of reducing expense, all claims may be brought in a single action.

The rules apply to any action in which, following the death of any person from personal injuries, damages are claimed by either:

   (i)   the executor of the deceased in respect of the relevant injuries; or

  (ii)   any relative of the deceased in respect of the death of the deceased.

"Relative" includes:

   (i)   the spouse of the deceased;

  (ii)   any person who was living with the deceased as husband or wife;

 (iii)   a parent or child of the deceased;

 (iv)   any person who was accepted by the deceased as a child of his family;

  (v)   any ascendant or descendant (other than a parent or child) of the deceased;

 (vi)   any person who, having been a spouse of the deceased, has ceased to be so by virtue of a divorce.

2. Intimation to persons having a title to sue (r 145)

The executor of the deceased or any one of the relatives mentioned in r 144 could raise an action for damages without reference to any other person with a title to sue.

This rule places an onus on the pursuer to state in the initial writ:
(i) that he is the only person with a title to sue the defender; or
(ii) that there are other persons having a title to sue the defender (in which case the pursuer must name and design such persons); or
(iii) that there are other persons having a title to sue the defender but whose names or whereabouts are unknown to the pursuer and cannot be reasonably ascertained.

If any person having a title to sue the defender is identified in the initial writ, the sheriff will order a notice in terms of Form CC in the schedule to the rules to be served on every such person. In addition the sheriff may order such advertisement or intimation to such persons as he deems appropriate.

3. Applications to sist as additional pursuer (r 146)

Any person who has received notice as described in r 145 above, may apply to be sisted as an additional pursuer in the action, in which case he must give notice of the application to all other parties in the action.

Rather than apply to be sisted as a pursuer, the person receiving intimation may opt to raise a separate action against the defender but, in that event, he would not be awarded the expenses of that action, except on cause shown.

4. Applications for interim payment of damages (r 147)

An order for an interim payment in an action of damages for personal injury may be made on an admission of liability by the defender, or if the sheriff is satisfied, on an assessment of the written pleadings and having heard parties, that the pursuer would be successful. Certain conditions have to be satisfied before an order for interim payment may be made.

In any action for damages for personal injury, the pursuer may at any time after the lodging of defences, apply for an interim payment of damages. The application is made by written motion served on the defender or defenders on a period of notice of 14 days.

If, after hearing parties on the motion, the sheriff is satisfied either:
- (i) that the defender or defenders have admitted liability; or
- (ii) that, if the action proceeded to proof, the pursuer would succeed on the question of liability without a substantial finding of contributory negligence and would obtain decree for damages,

the sheriff, if he is satisfied that the defender is:
- (i) insured in respect of the pursuer's claim; or
- (ii) a person whose means and resources are such as to enable him to make an interim payment,

may order the defender to make an interim payment to the pursuer of such an amount, not exceeding such reasonable proportion of the damages which in the opinion of the sheriff is likely to be recovered by the pursuer, as he deems appropriate.

Payment may be ordered in a lump sum or otherwise and is subject to the provisions of r 128 (payment of damages to persons under legal disability). A second or subsequent application may be made on cause shown by reason of a change of circumstances.

The provisions of the rule also apply to a counterclaim for damages for personal injury made by a defender.

"Personal injuries" include any disease or impairment of a person's physical or mental condition.

5. Final orders where interim payment made (r 148)

Any interim payment made under r 147 above is taken into account when the sheriff is giving effect to the defender's liability to the pursuer.

The pursuer may be ordered to repay to the defender any sum by which the interim payment exceeds the amount which the defender is liable to pay to the pursuer.

The sheriff may order any other defender or third party to make payment of any part of the interim payment which the defender who made it is entitled to recover from that other defender or third party by way of contribution or indemnity or in respect of any remedy or relief related to or connected with the pursuer's claim.

Appendix

Forms

131

Form A: Initial writ (r 3)

SHERIFFDOM OF   AT

A.B. *(design him; if he sues in any special capacity set that forth)*,
Pursuer

Against

C.D *(design him; if sued in any special capacity set that forth)*, Defender

The Pursuer craves the Court *(here set forth the specific decree, warrant or order asked)*

Condescendence

(State in numbered paragraphs the facts which form the ground of action)

Pleas-in-law

(State in numbered sentences)

(To be signed) A.B Pursuer;

or

X.Y. *(add designation and business address)*

Solicitor for Pursuer.

Form B: Warrant of citation (r 5(1))

(Place and date) Grants warrant to cite the defender by serving a copy of the writ and warrant upon a period of notice of   days, and appoints him, if he intends to defend, to lodge a notice of intention to defend with the sheriff clerk at

within the said period of notice after such service (and grants warrant to arrest on the dependence). (Meantime grants interim interdict, or warrant to arrest on the dependence, or sequestrates and grants warrant to inventory; or otherwise, as the case may be and to arrest to found jurisdiction).

Form B1: Warrant of citation: consistorial action (r 5(2))

19

Grants warrant to cite the defender   by serving   a copy of the writ and warrant upon a period of notice of   days, and appoints

if he intends to defend, or to dispute any claim made or make any claim to lodge the appropriate document with the Sheriff Clerk at

. *(Meantime grants interim interdict, or warrant to arrest on the dependence as the case may be.)*

Form B2: Warrant of citation: summary application (r 5(3))

(Place and date) Grants warrant to cite the defender (or respondent) by serving a copy of the writ and warrant upon a period of notice of days, and appoints him to answer within the Sheriff Court House at (in Room No, or in Chambers, *or as the case may be*), on the   day of   at   o'clock   noon, under certification of being held as confessed. *(Where necessary add* [meantime sequestrates and grants warrant to inventory and secure]; or [grants warrant to arrest on the dependence]; *or otherwise as the case may be).*

Form C: Citation (r 9)

A.B., Pursuer against C.D., Defender   Court Ref No
(Place and date) C.D., defender. You are hereby served with this copy writ and warrant, and required to answer thereto, conform to the said warrant.
IF YOU WISH TO DEFEND THIS ACTION you must lodge a notice of intention to defend with the Sheriff Clerk at   within days after this date and at the same time present this copy initial writ.
IF YOU DO NOTHING IN ANSWER TO THIS DOCUMENT the court may regard you as admitting the claim made against you and the pursuer may obtain decree against you in your absence.
[To be signed]
P.Q., Sheriff Officer, or
X.Y. *(add designation and business address)*
Solicitor for Pursuer

Form CC: Intimation to persons having a title to sue (r 145(2))

(Place, date)
Take notice that an action has been raised in   Sheriff Court *(address)* by *(name and design)* against *(name and design)*. It is believed

that you may have a title or interest to sue the said *(name)* in an action based upon [the injuries from which the late *(name and design)* died] or [the death of the late *(name and design)*]. You may therefore be entitled to enter this action as an additional pursuer. If you wish to do so, you may apply to the Sheriff at the above-mentioned Sheriff Court to be sisted as an additional pursuer within 14 days after the expiry of days from the date of service hereof. In the event of your making such an application you are required to serve notice of it on all of the parties to the action.

The date of service hereof is reckoned as commencing on the day of posting.

Solicitor for Pursuer

Form C1: Consistorial action (r 9)

Court Ref No

A.B., Pursuer against C.D., Defender

(Place and date) You are hereby served with this writ and warrant, and required to answer thereto conform to the said warrant.

IF YOU WISH TO DEFEND THIS ACTION or IF YOU WISH TO MAKE ANY CLAIM you should consult a solicitor with a view to lodging the appropriate document with the Sheriff Clerk at within 14 days after this date and at the same time present this copy initial writ.

IF YOU DO NOTHING IN ANSWER TO THIS DOCUMENT the Court may regard you as admitting the claim made against you and the pursuer may obtain decree against you in your absence.

(To be signed)   E.F. Sheriff Officer or

           G.H. *(Add designation and business address)*, Solicitor for Pursuer

Form D: Certificate of citation (r 9(2))

(Place and date)

I,   hereby certify that upon the day of   I duly cited C.D., the defender, to answer to the foregoing writ. This I did by *(set forth mode of service, if by officer and not by post, add* in presence of L.M. [design him], witness hereto with me subscribing). *In actions of divorce and separation also set forth any forms sent in accordance with Rule 131.*

(To be signed)   P.Q. Sheriff Officer
L.M. Witness or
X.Y. *(add designation and business address)*, Solicitor for Pursuer

Form E: Advertisement (r 11)

Court Ref No:

An action has been raised in   Sheriff Court by A.B. pursuer calling as a defender C.D. whose last known address was   .
If the said C.D wishes to defend the action or to make any claim therein he/she should immediately contact the Sheriff Clerk *(address)* from whom he/she may obtain the service copy initial writ.

X.Y *(add designation and business address)*
Solicitor for Pursuer or
P.Q. Sheriff Officer

Form E1: Display on the Walls of Court (r 11(1)(b))

Court Ref No:

An Action has been raised in   Sheriff Court by A.B. pursuer calling as a defender C.D. whose last known address was
If C.D wishes to defend the action or to make any claim therein he/she should immediately contact the Sheriff Clerk (address) from whom he/she may obtain the service copy initial writ.

Tel No:
(Signed) Sheriff Clerk
Date: *(insert date)*

Form F: Notice of intention to defend (r 33)

(Place and date) - C.D. *(design him)* Defender, intends to defend the action against him (and others) at the instance of A.B. *(design him)*.

C.D. Defender or
X.Y *(add address)*, Defender's Solicitor

Form G: Third party notice (r 50(4))

Third Party Notices in the Cause between
A.B., Pursuer and C.D., Defender
E.F., Third Party
To E.F.
This Notice is served upon you by the above named C.D. by virtue of
an order granted by Sheriff   in the action in which
the above-named A.B. is the pursuer and C.D. the defender. In the
action the pursuer claims against the defender £   in respect
of *(or otherwise as the case may be)* as more fully appears in the copy
initial writ and defences *(or copy record in the action)* enclosed herewith.

The defender denies any liability but maintains that if there is any
liability he shares that liability with you, as more fully appears from
his defences lodged in the above action and enclosed herewith.
(Or otherwise as the case may be)

And take notice that if you wish to resist either the claim of the
pursuer against the defender, or the claim of the defender against you,
you must lodge answers in the action not later than
being the date appointed by the Court for the regulation of further
procedure and must appear or be represented in court on that date,
otherwise the Court may pronounce such decree against you as it thinks
fit.

Dated this   day of   19
(Signed)   Solicitor for the Defender

Form H: Notice to additional defender (r 64(1))

To *(designation and address)*   Court Ref No
Take notice that in the action in which A.B. is the Pursuer and C.D. is
the Defender, in copies of the (initial writ and defences) (closed record)
which are herewith enclosed, your name has, by order of the Court dated
                , been added/substituted as a Defender to the
said action; and the action, originally directed against the said C.D. is
directed against you.
IF YOU WISH TO DEFEND THIS ACTION you must lodge defences
thereto with the Sheriff Clerk at   within
                days from the date of service hereof.
IF YOU DO NOTHING IN ANSWER TO THIS DOCUMENT the Court may
regard you as admitting the claim made against you and the Pursuer may

proceed and obtain decree against you in your absence.

(Date)   (Signed) P.Q. Sheriff Officer; or
                                          X.Y. *(add designation, and business
                                          address)*, Solicitor for Pursuer (or
                                          Defender)

Form H1: Form of intimation to alleged adulterer in action of divorce or separation (r 130(1)(a))

To *(name and address as in the Warrant)*
Take note that in an action number *('A' number)*, you are alleged to have committed adultery. A copy of the Initial Writ is attached. If you wish to dispute the truth of the allegation made against you, you may lodge a minute with the Sheriff Clerk *(insert full address of Sheriff Clerk)* for leave to appear as a party. Your minute must be lodged within (14) days from *(insert date)*, the date of posting of this intimation.

Date:- *(insert date)*   *(Signed)* A.B.
                                          (Solicitor for Pursuer)

NOTE: The minute to be lodged with the Sheriff Clerk must be in proper form. You should crave to be sisted as a party to the action and seek leave to lodge defences or answers. The minute must be accompanied by the appropriate fee of (£   ).

It may be in your best interests to consult a solicitor who, if necessary, will advise you on the availability of legal aid.

Form H2: Form of intimation to person with whom an improper association is alleged to have occurred (r 130(2)(b))

To *(name and address as in the Warrant)*
Take note that in an action number *('A' number)*, the defender is alleged to have had an improper association with you. A copy of the Initial Writ is attached. If you wish to dispute the truth of the allegation made against you, you may lodge a minute with the Sheriff Clerk *(insert full address of Sheriff Clerk)* for leave to appear as a party. Your minute must be lodged within [14] days from *(insert date)*, the date of posting of this intimation.

Date:- *(insert date)*   *(Signed)* A.B
                                          (Solicitor for Pursuer)

NOTE: The minute to be lodged with the Sheriff Clerk must be in proper form. You should crave to be sisted as a party to the action and seek leave to lodge defences or answers. The minute must be accompanied by the appropriate fee of (£   ).

It may be in your best interests to consult a solicitor who, if necessary, will advise you on the availability of legal aid.

Form H3: Form of intimation to a local authority or third party who may be liable to maintain a child (r 130(4))

To *(name and address as in the Warrant)*

Take note that in an action number *('A' number)*, the Court may make an order in respect of the custody of *(name and address)* a child in your care (or liable to be maintained by you). A copy of the Initial Writ is attached. If you wish to appear as a party, you may lodge a minute with the Sheriff Clerk *(insert full address of Sheriff Clerk)*, for leave to do so. Your minute must be lodged within [14] days from *(insert date)*, the date of posting of this intimation.

Date:-   *(insert date)*   *(Signed)* A.B.

(Solicitor for Pursuer)

NOTE: The minute to be lodged with the Sheriff Clerk must be in proper form. You should crave to be sisted as a party to the action and seek leave to lodge defences or answers. The minute must be accompanied by the appropriate fee of (£   ).

It may be in your best interests to consult a solicitor who, if necessary, will advise you on the availability of legal aid.

Form H4: Form of intimation to additional spouse of either party in proceedings relating to a polygamous marriage (r 130(5))

To *(name and address as in the Warrant)*

Take note that an action for divorce (*or* separation) number *('A' number)*, involves *(name and designation)* your spouse. A copy of the Initial Writ is attached. If you wish to appear as a party, you may lodge a minute with the Sheriff Clerk *(insert full address of Sheriff Clerk)*, for leave to do so. Your minute must be lodged within [14] days from *(insert date)*, the date of posting of this intimation.

Date:- *(insert date)*   *(Signed)* A.B.
                                                            (Solicitor for Pursuer)

NOTE : The minute to be lodged with the Sheriff Clerk must be in proper form. You should crave to be sisted as a party to the action and seek leave to lodge defences or answers. The minute must be accompanied by the appropriate fee of (£   ).

It may be in your best interests to consult a solicitor who, if necessary, will advise you on the availability of legal aid.

Form H5: Form of intimation to person having de facto custody of children (r 130(6))

To *(name and address as in the Warrant)*

Take note that in an action number *("A" number)*, the court may make an order in respect of the custody of *(name and address)* a child/children at present in your custody. A copy of the Initial Writ is attached. If you wish to appear as a party, you may lodge a minute with the Sheriff Clerk *(insert full address of Sheriff Clerk)*, for leave to do so. Your minute must be lodged within [14] days from *(insert date)*, the date of posting of this intimation.

Date:- *(insert date)*   *(Signed)* A.B.
                                                            (Solicitor for Pursuer)

NOTE: The minute to be lodged with the Sheriff Clerk must be in proper form. You should crave to be sisted as a party to the action and seek leave to lodge defences or answers. The minute must be accompanied by the appropriate fee of (£   ).

It may be in your best interests to consult a solicitor who, if necessary, will advise you on the availability of legal aid.

Form H6: Form of intimation to local authority or third party to whom care of a child is to be given (r 130(7)(a))

To *(name and address as in the Warrant)*

Take note that in an action number *('A' number)*, the court proposes to commit to your care the child *(name and address)*. A copy of the Initial Writ is attached. If you wish to appear as a party, you may lodge a minute with the Sheriff Clerk *(insert full address of Sheriff Clerk)*, for leave to do so. Your minute must be lodged within [14] days from *(insert date)*, the date of posting of this intimation.

Date:- *(insert date)*   *(Signed)* A.B.

                                                         (Solicitor for Pursuer)

NOTE: The minute to be lodged with the Sheriff Clerk must be in proper form. You should crave to be sisted as a party to the action and seek leave to lodge defences or answers. The minute must be accompanied by the appropriate fee of (£   ).

It may be in your best interests to consult a solicitor who, if necessary, will advise you on the availability of legal aid.

Form H6A: Form of intimation to local authority of supervision order (r 130(7)(b))

Initial Writ
in

A.B. *(Address)*   Pursuer (s)

against

C.D. *(Address)*   Defender(s)

To *(name and address of local authority)*

TAKE NOTICE

That on *(date)* in the Sheriff Court at *(place)* the Sheriff made a supervision order under *section 12 of the Matrimonial Proceedings (Children) Act 1958/* section 11(1)(b) of the Guardianship Act 1973, placing the child *(name and address)* under your supervision. A certified copy of the sheriff's interlocutor is attached hereto.

Date:- *(insert date)*   *(Signed)* A.B.

                                                         Sheriff Clerk

*Delete as appropriate

Form H7: Form of intimation to creditor in application for order for the transfer of property under section 8 of the Family Law (Scotland) Act 1985 (r 130(9))

To *(name and address as in the Warrant)*

Take note that in an action number *('A' number)* an order is sought for the transfer of property *(specify the order)*, over which you hold a security. A copy of the Initial Writ is attached. If you wish to appear as a party, you may lodge a minute with the Sheriff Clerk *(insert full address of Sheriff Clerk)* for leave to do so. Your minute must be lodged within [14] days from *(insert date)*, the date of posting this intimation.

Date:-   *(insert date)*   *(Signed)* A.B.
                                                    (Solicitor for Pursuer)

NOTE: The minute to be lodged with the Sheriff Clerk must be in proper form. You should crave to be sisted as a party to the action and seek leave to lodge defences or answers. The minute must be accompanied by the appropriate fee of (£   ).

It may be in your best interests to consult a solicitor who, if necessary, will advise you on the availability of legal aid.

Form I : Citation (r 75(1))

K.L. *(design him)*, you are required to attend at
Sheriff Court on   19   at   as a witness
for the   in the action at the instance of A.B. *(design him)*,
against C.D. *(design him)* (and to bring with you [*specify documents*]).
If you fail to attend without reasonable excuse having demanded and been paid your travelling expenses you may be ordered to pay a penalty not exceeding £250 and warrant may be granted for your arrest.

(Date)   (Signed) P.Q. Sheriff Officer; or
                                    X.Y. *(add designation and business address)*
                                    Solicitor for Pursuer (or Defender)

Note: Within certain specified limits claims for necessary outlays and loss of earnings will be met. Claims should be made to the person who has cited you to attend court and proof of any loss of earnings should be given to that person. If you wish your travelling expenses to be paid prior to your attendance you should apply to the person who has cited you.

Form J: Certificate of citation (r 75(1))

I certify that on   19   I duly cited K.L.
(design him) to attend at   Sheriff Court on
                19   at   as a witness for the
                in the action at the instance of A.B. *(design him)* against
E.F. *(design him)* [and I required him to bring with him *(specify*

documents)]. This I did *(set forth mode of citation)*.
(Date) (Signed) P.Q. Sheriff Officer; or
X.Y. *(add designation and business address)*
Solicitor for Pursuer (or Defender)

Form K: Notice in optional procedure for commission and diligence (r 81(1))

Order by the Sheriff Court at
In the cause *(Reference No)*
in which
A.B. *(design)* is Pursuer and
C.D. *(design)* is Defender
To *(name and designation of party or parties or haver, from whom the documents are sought to be recovered)*
Take notice that you are hereby required to produce to the sheriff clerk at
within seven days of the service upon
you of this order -

(1) this order itself which must be produced intact;
(2) a certificate signed and completed in terms of the form appended hereto; and
(3) all documents in your possession falling within the specification enclosed herewith, together with a list or inventory of such documents signed by you as relative to this order and your certificate.

Production may be made either by lodging the above at the said office of the sheriff clerk, or by registered or recorded delivery letter or registered postal packet enclosing the same, and addressed to the said sheriff clerk at said office.
(Signature and business address of the solicitor of the party in whose favour commission and diligence has been granted)
(Date)
Note: If you claim confidentiality for any of the documents produced by you, such documents must nevertheless be produced, but may be placed in a special enclosure by themselves, marked "confidential".

CERTIFICATE
I hereby certify with reference to the order of the sheriff court at
in the cause *(Reference No)* and the

relative specification of documents, served upon me and marked respectively X.Y. -

    (1) that the documents which are produced and which are enumerated in the inventory signed by me and marked Z, are the whole documents in my possession falling under the specification.

or   that I have no documents in my possession falling within the specification.

    (2) that, to the best of my knowledge and belief, there are in existence other documents falling within the specification, but not in my possession, namely *(describe them by reference to one or more of the descriptions of documents in the specification)*, which were last seen by me on or about *(date)*, at *(place)*, in the hands of *(name and address of the person).*

or   that I know of the existence of no documents in the possession of any person, other than myself, which fall within the specification.

(Signed)

Form L: Notice of removal (r 104)

To *(name, designation, and address of party in possession).*
You are required to remove from *(describe subjects)* at the term of *(or if different terms, state them and the subjects to which they apply)*, in terms of lease *(describe it)* or (in terms of your letter of removal of date
) *(or otherwise as the case may be).*

Form M: Letter of removal (r 104)

To *(name and designation of addressee)*
(Place and date) I am to remove from *(state subjects by usual name of short description sufficient for identification)* at the term of
                K.L. *(add designation and address).*
If not holograph to be attested thus -
                M.N. *(add designation and address),*
                witness.

Form N: Notice of removal under s 37 of 1907 Act (r 105)

To K.L. *(designation and address).*
You are required to remove from
that portion of ground *(describe it);* or the mill of *(describe it);* or the
shootings of the lands and estate of *(describe them)*; or *(other subjects to
which this notice is applicable),* at the term of Whitsunday *(insert year)
(or Martinmas, as the case may be, inserting after the year the words,
being the 15th day of May, or the 11th day of November, or the 28th
day of May, or the 28th day of November, as the case may be).*

Form O: Notice of appearance (r 117)

A.B. Pursuer against C.D., E.F., and G.H. Defenders
Court Ref No

(Place and date) - C.D. *(design him)*, defender, intends to appear in the
above action and lodge *defences to the competency of the action.
*objections to the condescendence of the fund *in medio*
*a claim on the fund *in medio.*
(Signed)   C.D., Defender or
                            X.Y. *(add designation and business address)*
                            Solicitor for Defender
*delete as appropriate

Form P: Receipt (r 128(4))

In the Sheriff Court of   at
Receipt for a Payment into Court
In the cause, matter or proceeding *(state names of parties or other
appropriate description)*
(Place and Date)
A.B. *(design him)* has this day paid into Court the sum of £
being a payment into Court in terms of Rule 141 money which in an
action of damages, has become payable to a person under legal
disability.
(Note) If the payment is made under Rule 141(2) add "the custody of
which money has been accepted at the request of *(name of Court making
request)."*

(Signed)   Sheriff Clerk

N.B. The person paying the money into Court is required to complete and transmit the subjoined Form Q to the Secretary of State, forthwith. TO BE PERFORATED.

Form Q: Letter intimating payment (r 128(4))

(Address)   (Date)

To The Secretary of State

Sir,

I/We paid into the Sheriff Court at

on   19   , the sum of

in the *(State name of cause, matter or proceeding)*.

Yours faithfully

(Signature)

Form R: Additional particulars for receipt (r 128(4))

The above-mentioned payment into Court was:-

(a) Lodged on Deposit Receipt No   with the *(state name of Bank)* pending the Orders of the Court.

(b) Deposited in the National Savings Bank, Account No

(c) *(Otherwise as the case may be, stating similar particulars)*.

Name and address of Solicitor (or Insurance Company) representing the person who made the payment into Court:-

                          (Date)

                          (Signed)   Sheriff Clerk

Form S: Form of notice to defender where it is stated he consents to the granting of decree of separation and aliment (r 131)

TAKE NOTICE that the copy initial writ served on you together with this Notice states that you consent to the grant of decree of separation -

1. If you do so consent the consequences to you are that -

     (a) provided the pursuer establishes the fact that there has been no cohabitation between the parties to the marriage at any time during a continuous period of two years after the date of the marriage and immediately preceding the bringing of this action and you consent, a decree of separation will be granted;

(b) on the grant of decree of separation you will be obliged to live apart from the pursuer but the marriage will continue to subsist; a husband will continue to have a legal obligation to support his wife and children;

(c) apart from these consequences there may be others applicable to you depending upon your particular circumstances.

2. If you do consent to the grant of decree you may apply to the Court in this action -

(a) for payment by the pursuer to you of aliment; and

(b) for an order providing for access to or the custody, maintenance and education of any child of the marriage, or any child accepted as such, who is under 16 years of age.

3. In order to make such an application to the Court you require to give notice in the appropriate form to the Court. If you wish to make such an application you should consult a solicitor.

4. If after considering the foregoing, you wish to consent to decree, you should complete and sign the attached Form of Notice of Consent and send it to the Sheriff Clerk at the Sheriff Court referred to in the initial writ within 14 days of the date of this Notice.

5. If after consenting you wish to withdraw your consent you must immediately inform the Sheriff Clerk at the Sheriff Court referred to in the initial writ in writing that you withdraw your consent to decree being granted against you in the action at the instance of *(insert name and address of your husband or wife as the case may be).*

(Date)   (Signed)

                               (Signature of Pursuer or his Agent)

Form S1: Form of notice to defender where it is stated he consents to the granting of decree of divorce (r 131)

TAKE NOTICE that the copy initial writ served on you together with the Notice states that you consent to grant of decree of divorce.

1. If you do so consent the consequences to you are that -

(a) provided the pursuer establishes the fact that there has been no cohabitation between the parties to the marriage at any time during a continuous period of two years after the date of the marriage and immediately preceding the bringing of this action and that you consent, a decree will be granted;

(b) on the grant of a decree of divorce you may lose your rights of succession to the pursuer's estate;

(c) decree of divorce will end the marriage thereby affecting any right to such pension as may depend upon marriage continuing or upon your being left a widow; the State widow's pension will not be payable to you when the pursuer dies;

(d) apart from these consequences there may be others applicable to you depending upon your particular circumstances.

2. If you do consent to the grant of decree you are still entitled to apply to the Sheriff in this action -

    (a) to make financial provision for you under the Divorce (Scotland) Act 1976 by making an order -

    (i) for the payment by the pursuer to you of a periodical allowance;

    (ii) for the payment by the pursuer to you of a capital sum;

    (iii) varying the terms of any marriage settlement.

    (b) to make an order providing for the custody, maintenance and education of any child of the marriage, or any child accepted as such, who is under 16 years of age.

3. In order to make such an application to the Sheriff you require to give notice in the appropriate form to the Court. If you wish to make such an application you should consult a solicitor.

4. If after considering the foregoing you wish to consent to decree you should complete and sign the attached Form of Notice of Consent, and send it to the Sheriff Clerk at the Sheriff Court referred to in the initial writ, within 14 days of the receipt of this Notice.

5. If after consenting you wish to withdraw your consent you must immediately inform the Sheriff Clerk at the Sheriff Court referred to in the initial writ in writing that you withdraw your consent to decree being granted against you in the action at the instance of *(insert name and address of your husband or wife as the case may be)*.

Form S2: Form of notice to defender in an action of separation and aliment where it is stated there has been five years' non-cohabitation (r 131)

1. TAKE NOTICE that the copy initial writ served on you together

with this Notice states that there has been no cohabitation between you and the pursuer at any time during a continuous period of five years after the date of the marriage and immediately preceding the commencement of this action and that if the pursuer establishes this as a fact and the Court is satisfied that there are grounds justifying decree of separation a decree will be granted, unless in the opinion of the Court the grant of decree would result in grave financial hardship to you.

2. On the grant of decree of separation you will be obliged to live apart from the pursuer but the marriage will continue to subsist. A husband will continue to have a legal obligation to support his wife and children.

3. You are entitled, whether or not you dispute that there has been no such cohabitation during such a period, to apply to the Sheriff in this action -
   (a) if you are the wife, for payment by the pursuer to you of aliment; and
   (b) for an order providing for the custody, maintenance and education of any child of the marriage, or any child accepted as such, who is under 16 years of age.

4. In order to make such an application you require to give notice in the appropriate form to the Court. If you wish to make such an application you should consult a solicitor.

Form S3: Form of notice to defender in an action of divorce where it is stated there has been five years' non-cohabitation (r 131)

1. TAKE NOTICE that the copy initial writ served on you together with this Notice states that there has been no cohabitation between you and the pursuer at any time during a continuous period of five years after the date of the marriage and immediately preceding the commencement of this action and that if the pursuer establishes this as a fact and the Court is satisfied that the marriage has broken down irretrievably a decree will be granted, unless in the opinion of the Court the grant of decree would result in grave financial hardship to you.

2. Decree of divorce will end the marriage thereby affecting any right to such pension as may depend upon the marriage continuing or upon your being left a widow, the State widow's pension will not be

payable to you when the pursuer dies. You may also lose your rights of succession to the pursuer's estate.
3. You are entitled, whether or not you dispute that there has been no such cohabitation during such a period, to apply to the Sheriff in this action -
   (a) to make financial provision for you under the Divorce (Scotland) Act 1976 by making an order -
      (i) for the payment by the pursuer to you of a periodical allowance;
      (ii) for the payment by the pursuer to you of a capital sum;
      (iii) varying the terms of any marriage settlement;
   (b) to make an order providing for the custody, maintenance and education of any child of the marriage or of any child accepted as such, who is under 16 years of age.
4. In order to make such an application you require to give notice in the appropriate form to the Court. If you wish to make such an application you should consult a solicitor.

Form T: Form of notice of consent in actions of divorce and of separation under section 1(2)(d) of the Divorce (Scotland) Act 1976 (r 131)

I (*full name and address of the defender to be inserted by the pursuer or the pursuer's solicitor before sending Notice*) have received a copy of the initial writ in the action against me at the instance of (*full name and address of pursuer to be inserted by him or his solicitor before sending Notice*)
I understand that it states that I consent to the grant of decree (of divorce or of separation and aliment) in this action.
I have considered the consequences to be mentioned in the Notice sent together with this Notice.
I consent to the grant of decree (of divorce or of separation and aliment) in this action.
(Dated)   (Signed)
                     Defender   Witness

Form T1: Form of consent of parent or guardian in proceedings for custody of children under section 47 of the Children Act 1975 (r 3(8))

In

Pursuer(s)
Defender(s)

I, *(name and address)*

confirm that I am the mother/father/guardian/tutor/curator* of the child *(insert full name of the child as it is given on the birth certificate, and the child's present address)*

I understand that if I consent to the granting of custody to the pursuer(s), the care, possession and control of the child may be granted to the pursuer(s) by the court.

I hereby consent to the making of a custody order in relation to the child *(name of child)* in favour of *(name and address of pursuer(s)*

Dated at *(place)* the   day of   19

Signature of person consenting

Signature of Witness

Full Name

Designation

Address

Signature of Witness

Full Name

Designation

Address

*Delete whichever is inappropriate

Form T2: Notice to local authority under section 49(1) of the Children Act 1975 of presentation of an initial writ for custody of a child under section 47 of that Act (r 130(9))

Initial Writ

in

A.B. *(address)*   Pursuer(s)

for

Custody of the child E.F.

To *(name and address)*

TAKE NOTICE

1. That the pursuer has presented an initial writ to the Sheriff Court at

(address) for the custody of the child E.F. A copy of the writ is attached to this notice.

2. That you are required under section 49(2) of the Children Act 1975 to submit to the court a report on all the circumstances of the child and on the proposed arrangements for the care and upbringing of the child.

Dated the   day of   19

                        (Signed)
                        (Address)
                        (Solicitor for the pursuer)

Form U: Request for preliminary ruling of the Court of Justice of the European Communities (r 134(3))

(Here set out a statement of the case for the European Court, giving brief particulars of the case and issues between the parties, and relevant facts found by the Court, any relevant rules and provisions of Scots Law, and the relevant Treaty provisions, acts, instruments or rules of Community Law giving rise to the reference.)

The preliminary ruling of the Court of Justice of the European Communities is accordingly sought on the following questions - 1, 2, etc. *(Insert the questions on which the ruling is sought).*

Dated the   day of   19

Form V: Form of certificate by medical officer of hospital or similar institution (r 11A)

I *(Name and designation)* certify that, having had transmitted to me a copy initial writ in an action of divorce or of separation and aliment at the instance of *(name and designation)* Pursuer, against *(name and designation)* Defender,

(a) I have on the   day of   personally delivered a copy thereof to the said defender who is under my care at *(address)* and I have explained the contents or purport thereof to him (or her).

or

(b) I have not delivered a copy thereof to the said defender who is under my care at *(address)* and I have not explained the contents or purport thereof to him (or her) and that for the following reasons *(state reasons)*.

(Address and date)   *(Signature and designation)*

Form V1: Form of intimation to children, next of kin and curator bonis in an action of divorce or separation where the defender suffers from a mental disorder (r 11A(3))

To *(name and address as in the Warrant)*

Take note that an action of divorce (or separation) number *('A' number)* has been raised against *(name and designation)* your (father, mother, brother or other relative, or ward, as the case may be). A copy of the Initial Writ is attached. If you wish to appear as a party, you may lodge a minute with the Sheriff Clerk *(insert full address of Sheriff Clerk)*, for leave to do so. Your minute must be lodged within [14] days from *(insert date)*, the date of posting of this intimation.

Date:- *(insert date)*   *(Signed)* A.B

                    (Solicitor for Pursuer)

NOTE : The minute to be lodged with the Sheriff Clerk must be in proper form. You should crave to be sisted as a party to the action and seek leave to lodge defences or answers. The minute must be accompanied by the appropriate fee of (£   ).

It may be in your best interests to consult a solicitor who, if necessary, will advise you on the availability of legal aid.

Form V2: Form of intimation to children and next of kin in an action of divorce or separation where the defender's address is unknown (r 11A(3))

To *(name and address as in the Warrant)*

Take note that an action of divorce (or separation) number *('A' number)*, has been raised against *(name)* (your father, mother, brother or other relative *as the case may be)*. If you know of his/her present address, you are requested to forward the same to the Sheriff Clerk *(insert full address of Sheriff Clerk)* forthwith. You may also if you wish to appear as a party lodge a minute with the Sheriff Clerk for leave to do so. Your minute must be lodged within [14] days from *(insert date)*, the date of posting of this intimation.

Date:- *(insert date)*   *(Signed)* A.B.
                                                     (Solicitor for Pursuer)
NOTE: The minute to be lodged with the Sheriff Clerk must be in proper
form. You should crave to be sisted as a party to the action and seek
leave to lodge defences or answers. The minute must be accompanied
by the appropriate fee of (£   ).
It may be in your best interests to consult a solicitor who, if necessary,
will advise you on the availability of legal aid.

Form W: Form of transmission to medical officer of hospital or similar institution (r 11A)

To *(insert name and address)*
In accordance with the Sheriff Courts (Scotland) Act 1907 a copy of the
initial writ at the instance of *(name and address)* against *(name and
address)* is sent herewith and you are requested to deliver it personally to
the said   and to explain the contents or
purport thereof to him (or her) unless you are satisfied that such delivery
or explanation would be dangerous to his (or her) health or mental
condition. You are further requested to complete and return to me in the
enclosed stamped and addressed envelope the certificate appended hereto,
striking out what is not applicable.
(Address and date)   *(Solicitor for Pursuer)*

Form X: Minute for decree (r 72(5))

A.B. for the pursuer having considered the evidence contained in the
affidavits and the other documents all as specified in the Schedule hereto
and being satisfied that upon the evidence a motion for decree (in terms
of the crave of the initial writ) or (in such restricted terms as may be
appropriate) may properly be made, moves the court accordingly.
In respect whereof
(Signed)
(Designation)
SCHEDULE
(Number and specify documents considered)

Form Z: Extract decree of divorce (r 90A)

SHERIFF COURT
AT
The   day of   Nineteen hundred and
in an action of Divorce in the Sheriff Court of
at   at the instance of
Pursuer   Defender
who were married at *(place)* on *(date)*
The sheriff pronounced Decree
(1) divorcing the Defender from the Pursuer
(2) awarding custody to the Pursuer/Defender of the following child/children:
(3) ordaining payment:
  (a) by the   to the   of
      £   per   as aliment for each of said child/children until sixteen years of age:
  (b) by the Defender to the Pursuer of a perodical allowance of £
      per   payable until her death or remarriage:
  (c) by the Defender to the Pursuer of a capital sum of £
  (d) by the   to the   of £
      of expenses:
(4) finding the Defender liable to the Pursuer in expenses as the same may be subsequently taxed and decerned for:
(5) granting leave to any party showing interest to apply to the Court for any order required anent custody and aliment until   19
And the said Sheriff grants Warrant for all lawful execution hereon:
Extracted at   this   day of
19   by me
Sheriff Clerk of

Form SDA1: Application for divorce (with consent of other party to the marriage) husband and wife having lived apart for at least two years (r 136(1))

Under the Divorce (Scotland) Act 1976, Section 1 (2)(d) Simplified Procedure
Sheriff Clerk
Sheriff Court House

(Tel)

Before completing this form, you should have read the leaflet entitled "Do it yourself Divorce", which explains the circumstances in which a divorce may be sought by that method. If simplified procedure appears to suit your circumstances, you may use this form to apply for divorce.

Below you will find directions designed to assist you with your application. Please follow them carefully. In the event of difficulty, you may contact any Sheriff Clerk's Office or Citizens Advice Bureau or the Court of Session Divorce Section, Edinburgh.

Directions for making application
WRITE IN INK, USING BLOCK CAPITALS

Application (Part 1)	1.	Complete and sign Part 1 of the form (pages 3-7), paying particular attention to the notes opposite each section.
Consent of Husband/Wife (Part 2)	2.	When you have filled in Part 1 of the form, attach the (blue) Instruction Sheet SP3 to it and send both documents to your husband/wife for completion of the consent at Part 2 ([page 9]) NOTE: If your husband/wife does NOT complete and sign the form of consent, your application cannot proceed further under the simplified procedure. In that event, if you still wish to obtain a divorce, you should consult a solicitor.
Affidavit (Part 3)	3.	When the application has been returned to you with the Consent (Part 2) duly completed and signed, you should then take the form to a Justice of the Peace, Notary Public, Commissioner for Oaths or other duly authorised person so that your affidavit in Part 3 ([page 10]) can be completed and sworn.
Returning completed application form court	4.	When directions 1-3 above have been carried out, your application is now ready to be sent to the Court at the above address. With it you must enclose: (i) Your marriage certificate (the document headed "Extract of an entry in a Register of Marriages", which will be returned to you in due course), and (ii) Either a cheque or postal order in respect of the Court fee, crossed and made payable to "the Sheriff Clerk", or a completed form SP15,

claiming exemption from the Court fee.

5.   Receipt of your application will be promptly acknowledged. Should you wish to withdraw the application for any reason, please contact the Sheriff Clerk immediately.

WRITE IN INK, USING BLOCK CAPITALS

PART 1

1. NAME AND ADDRESS OF APPLICANT

Surname: Other name(s) in full:

Present address:

Daytime telephone number if any:

2. NAME AND ADDRESS OF HUSBAND /WIFE

Surname: Other name(s) in full:

Present address:

Daytime telephone number if any:

3. JURISDICTION

Please indicate with a tick (√) in the appropriate box or boxes which of the following apply:

PART A

(i)   I consider myself to be domiciled in Scotland   ☐

(ii)   I have lived in Scotland for a period of at least 12 months immediately before the date of signing this application   ☐

(iii) My husband/wife considers himself/herself to be domiciled in Scotland   ☐

(iv) My husband/wife has lived in Scotland for a period of at least 12 months immediately before the date of signing this application   ☐

PART B

(v)   I have lived at the address shown in Section 1 for at least 40 days immediately before the date I signed this application   ☐

(vi) My husband/wife has lived at the address shown in Section 2 for at least 40 days immediately before the date I signed this application   ☐

4. DETAILS OF PRESENT MARRIAGE

Place of Marriage: (Registration District)

Date of Marriage: Day   month   year

5.   PERIOD OF SEPARATION

(i)   Please state the date on which you ceased to live with your husband/wife. (If more than 2 and one half years, just give the month and year)   Day   Month   Year

(ii) Have you lived with your husband/wife since that date?
  (Tick (√) box which applies) □ YES NO □
(iii)If yes, for how long in total did you live together before
  finally separating again?   months
6. RECONCILIATION
Is there any reasonable prospect of reconciliation with your
husband/wife?
  (Tick (√) box which applies) □ YES NO □
Do you consider that the marriage has broken down irretrievably?
  (Tick (√) box which applies) □ YES NO □
7. CONSENT
Does your husband/wife consent to a divorce being granted?
  (Tick (√) box which applies) □ YES NO □
8. MENTAL DISABILITY
As far as you are aware is your husband/wife incapable of
managing his/her affairs because of a mental disorder
(whether illness or deficiency)?
  (Tick (√) box which applies) □ YES NO □
  (if yes, give details)
9. CHILDREN
Are there any children of the marriage under the age of 16?
  (Tick (√) box which applies) □ YES NO □
10. OTHER COURT ACTIONS
Are you aware of any court actions proceeding in any country (incuding
Scotland) which may affect your marriage?
  (Tick (√) box which applies) □ YES NO □
  (if yes, give details)
11. REQUEST FOR DIVORCE AND DISCLAIMER OF FINANCIAL
PROVISION
I confirm that the facts stated in Sections 1-10 above apply to my
marriage.
I do NOT ask the Court to make any financial awards in connection
with this application.
I request the Court to grant decree of divorce from my husband/wife.
(Date)   (Signature)
IMPORTANT - Part 1 MUST be completed, signed and dated before
sending the application form to your husband/wife.

PART 2
CONSENT BY APPLICANT'S HUSBAND/WIFE TO DIVORCE
NOTE: Before completing this Part of the form, please read the notes

opposite

I,   *(Full names, in BLOCK letters, of Applicant's husband/wife)*
residing at *(Address, also in BLOCK letters)*
HEREBY STATE THAT

a) I have read Part 1 of this application;
b) The Applicant has lived apart from me for a continuous period of two years immediately preceding the date of the application (Section 11 of Part 1);
c) I do not ask the Court to make any order for payment to me by the Applicant of a periodical allowance (i.e. a regular payment of money weekly or monthly, etc for maintenance);
d) I do not ask the Court to make any order for payment to me by the Applicant of a capital sum (i.e. a lump sum payment);
e) I understand that divorce may result in the loss to me of property rights; and
f) I CONSENT TO DECREE OF DIVORCE BEING GRANTED IN RESPECT OF THIS APPLICATION

(Date)   (Signature)

NOTE: You may withdraw your consent, even after giving it, at any time before divorce is granted by the Court. Should you wish to do so, you must immediately advise:

Address of Court
(Tel)

PART 3
APPLICANT'S AFFIDAVIT
To be completed only after Parts 1 and 2 have been signed and dated.

I,   *(insert Applicant's full name)*
     residing at *(insert Applicant's present home address)*
     Town   Country

SWEAR that to the best of my knowledge and belief:

(1) the facts stated in Part 1 of this Application are true; and
(2) the signature in Part 2 of this Application is that of my *husband/wife.

Signature of Applicant ....

[To be completed by Justice of the Peace, Notary Public or Commissioner for Oaths] -
SWORN at *(Place)*
this   day of   19
before me *(full name)*
(full address)

160

Signature ....
Justice of the Peace/Notary Public/Commissioner for Oaths*
*Delete as appropriate

Form SDA2: Application for divorce husband and wife having lived apart for at least five years (r 136(2))

Under the Divorce (Scotland) Act 1976, section 1(2)(e)
    Simplified Procedure
Sheriff Clerk
Sheriff Court House
(Tel)

Before completing this form, you should have read the leaflet entitled "Do it yourself Divorce", which explains the circumstances in which a divorce may be sought by that method. If the simplified procedure appears to suit your circumstances, you may use this form to apply for divorce.

Below you will find directions designed to assist you with your application. Please follow them carefully. In the event of difficulty, you may contact the Sheriff Clerk's Office or Citizens Advice Bureau or the Court of Session Divorce Section, Edinburgh.

Directions for making application
WRITE IN INK, USING BLOCK CAPITALS

Application (Part 1)	1. Complete and sign Part 1 of the form [pages 3-7] paying particular attention to the notes opposite each section.
Affidavits (Part 2)	2. When you have completed Part 1, you should take the form to a Justice of the Peace, Notary Public, Commissioner for Oaths or other duly authorised person so that your affidavit in Part 2 [page 8] can be completed and sworn.
Returning completed application form to Court	3. When directions 1 and 2 above have all been carried out, your application is now ready to be returned to the Sheriff Clerk at the above address. With it you must enclose :

(i) Your marriage certificate (the document headed "Extract of an entry in a Register of Marriages" which will be returned to you in due course) - check the notes on page [2] to see if you need to obtain a letter from the General Register Office stating that there is no record of your husband/wife having divorced you, and

(ii) Either a cheque or postal order in respect of the Court fee, crossed and made payable to "the Sheriff Clerk", or a completed form SP15, claiming exemption from the Court fee.

4. Receipt of your application will be promptly acknowledged. Should you wish to withdraw the application for any reason, please contact the Sheriff Clerk immediately.

PART 1

WRITE IN INK, USING BLOCK CAPITALS

1. NAME AND ADDRESS OF APPLICANT

Surname: Other name(s) in full:

Present address:

Daytime telephone number if any:

2. NAME OF HUSBAND /WIFE

Surname: Other name(s) in full:

3. ADDRESS OF HUSBAND /WIFE (If the address of your husband/wife is not known, please enter "not known" in this section and proceed to section 4)

Present address:

Daytime telephone number if any:

4. Only complete this section if you do not know the present address of your husband/wife

NEXT-OF-KIN

Name   Address

Relationship to your husband/wife:

CHILDREN OF THE MARRIAGE

Names and dates of birth   Addresses

If insufficient space is available to list all the children of the marriage, please continue on a separate sheet and attach to this form.

5. JURISDICTION

Please indicate with a tick (√) in the appropriate box or boxes which of the following apply:

PART A

   (i)   I consider myself to be domiciled in Scotland   ☐

   (ii) I have lived in Scotland for a period of at least 12 months immediately before the date of signing this application   ☐

   (iii) My husband/wife considers himself/herself to be domiciled in Scotland   ☐

(iv)My husband/wife has lived in Scotland for a period of at
    least 12 months immediately before the date of signing this
    application   ☐

PART B

(v) I have lived at the address shown in Section 1 for at least
    40 days immediately before the date I signed this
    application   ☐

(vi)My husband/wife has lived at the address shown in Section
    2 for at least 40 days immediately before the date I signed
    this application   ☐

6. DETAILS OF PRESENT MARRIAGE

Place of Marriage: (Registration District)

Date of Marriage: Day   month   year

7. PERIOD OF SEPARATION

(i) Please state the date on which you ceased to live with your
    husband/wife. (If more than 5 and one half years, just give the
    month and year)   Day   Month   Year

(ii) Have you lived with your husband/wife since that date?
        (Tick (√) box which applies) ☐ YES NO ☐

(iii)If yes, for how long in total did you live together before
    finally separating again?   months

8. RECONCILIATION

Is there any reasonable prospect of reconciliation with your
husband/wife?
        (Tick (√) box which applies) ☐ YES NO ☐

Do you consider that the marriage has broken down irretrievably?
        (Tick (√) box which applies) ☐ YES NO ☐

9. MENTAL DISABILITY

As far as you are aware is your husband/wife incapable of
managing his/her affairs because of a mental disorder
(whether illness or deficiency)?
        (Tick (√) box which applies) ☐ YES NO ☐
        (if yes, give details)

10. CHILDREN

Are there any children of the marriage under the age of 16?
        (Tick (√) box which applies) ☐ YES NO ☐

11. OTHER COURT ACTIONS

Are you aware of any court actions proceeding in any country (including
Scotland) which may affect your marriage?
        (Tick (√) box which applies) ☐ YES NO ☐
        (if yes, give details)

12. DECLARATION AND REQUEST FOR DIVORCE

I confirm that the facts stated in sections 1-11 above apply to my marriage.

I do NOT ask the Court to make any financial awards in connection with this application.

I believe that no grave financial hardship will be caused to my husband/wife as a result of granting this application.

I request the Court to grant decree of divorce from my husband/wife.

(Date)   (Signature)

IMPORTANT - Part 1 MUST be completed, signed and dated before sending the application form to your husband/wife.

PART 2

APPLICANT'S AFFIDAVIT

To be completed only after Part 1 has been signed and dated.

I,   *(insert Applicant's full name)*

residing at *(insert Applicant's present home address)*

Town   Country

SWEAR that to the best of my knowledge and belief the facts stated in Part 1 of this Application are true.

Signature of Applicant ....

[To be completed by Justice of the Peace, Notary Public or Commissioner for Oaths] -

SWORN at *(Place)*

this   day of   19

before me *(full name)*

(full address)

Signature ....

Justice of the Peace/Notary Public/Commissioner for Oaths*

*Delete as appropriate

Form SDA3: Consent to application for divorce husband and wife having lived apart for at least two years (r 136(3))

Under the Divorce (Scotland) Act 1976, section 1(2)(d)

Simplified Procedure

In Part 1 of the enclosed form your husband/wife is applying for divorce on the ground that the marriage has broken down irretrievably because you and (s)he have lived apart for at least two years AND you consent to the divorce being granted.

Such consent must be given formally in writing at Part 2 of the application form. BEFORE completing that part, you are requested to read it over carefully so that you understand the effects of consenting to divorce. Thereafter -

If you wish to consent

(a) Check the details given by the applicant at Part 1 of the form to ensure that they are correct to the best of your knowledge;

(b) Complete Part 2 (Form of Consent) by entering your name and address at the appropriate place and adding your signature and the date; and

(c) Return the whole application form to your husband/wife at the address given in Part 1.

Once your husband/wife has completed the remainder of the form and has submitted it to the Court, a copy of the whole application (including your consent) will later be served upon you formally by the Court.

In the event of the divorce being granted, you will automatically be sent a copy of the extract decree. (Should you change your address before receiving the copy extract decree, please notify the Court immediately).

If you do NOT wish to consent

Please return the application form, with Part 2 uncompleted, to your husband/wife and advise him/her of your decision.

The Court will NOT grant a divorce under this application if Part 2 of the form is not completed by you.

Sheriff Clerk

Sheriff Court

Form SDA4: Citation in section 1(2)(e) cases (r 138(1))

Under the Divorce (Scotland) Act 1976 section 1(2)(e) Simplified Procedure

M   19

APPLICATION FOR DIVORCE

HUSBAND AND WIFE HAVING LIVED APART FOR AT LEAST FIVE YEARS

Your husband/wife has applied to the Court for divorce on the ground that the marriage has broken down irretrievably *because you and (s)he have lived apart for a period of at least five years.*

A copy of the application is hereby served upon you.

1. Please note:
   (a) that the Court may not make financial awards under this procedure and that your husband/wife is making no claim against you for payment of a periodical allowance (i.e. regular payment of money weekly, monthly etc for his/her maintenance) or a capital sum (i.e. lump sum).
   (b) that your husband/wife states that you will not suffer financial hardship in the event of decree of divorce being granted.
2. Divorce may result in the loss to you of property rights (e.g. the right to succeed to the Applicant's estate on his/her death) or the right, where appropriate, to a widow's pension.
3. If you wish to oppose the granting of a divorce, you should put your reasons in writing and send your letter to the address shown below. Your letter must reach the Court before
4. In the event of the divorce being granted, you will be sent a copy of the extract decree.

(Should you change your address before receiving the copy extract decree, please notify the Court immediately).

Sheriff Clerk/ Sheriff Officer

Sheriff Clerk, Sheriff Court House

(Tel)

EXPLANATORY NOTE: If you wish to exercise your right to claim a financial award you should immediately advise the Court that you oppose the application for that reason, and thereafter consult a solicitor.

Form SDA5: Extract decree (r 141(1))

SHERIFF COURT

At   the   day of

Nineteen hundred and

in an action in the Sheriff Court of

at   at the instance of   Applicant

                                        Respondent

who were married at *(place)* on *(date)*

the Sheriff pronounced decree divorcing the Respondent from the Applicant

Extracted at   the   day of

Nineteen Hundred and   by me Sheriff Clerk of
Sheriff Clerk

Form SDA6: Form of intimation for display on Walls of Court (r 138(9))

Court Ref No:

An application for divorce has been made in
Sheriff Court by A.B. calling as defender C.D.
If C.D wishes to oppose the granting of decree of divorce he/she should immediately contact the Sheriff Clerk from whom he/she may obtain a copy of the application.
Tel No:-
(Signed) Sheriff Clerk
Date:- *(insert date)*

Form SDA7: Form of intimation to children and next of kin in simplified divorce application (r 138(10)

To *(Name and address)*
TAKE NOTICE that an application for divorce *(number of application)* has been made against *(name of respondent)* your (father, mother, brother or other relative *as the case may be*). A copy of the application is attached. If you know of his/her present address you are requested to forward it to the Sheriff Clerk *(insert full address of Sheriff Clerk)* forthwith. You may also, if you wish, oppose the granting of decree of divorce by sending a letter to the court giving your reasons for your opposition to the application. Your letter must be sent to the Sheriff Clerk within [14] days from *(insert date)*, the date of posting of this intimation.
Date:- *(insert date)*
(Signed) A.B.
Sheriff Clerk
NOTE: It may be in your best interests to consult a solicitor, who if necessary, will advise you on the availability of legal aid.

Index

INDEX

INDEX